Other Books by Dephne

Incorruptible Beauty

Breaking Soul Ties

A Woman's Body Is A Temple

A Woman's Body Is A Temple: Study Guide & Self Reflection

The Art of Being Private: Building In Silence

Copyright

Dedication

This book is dedicated to my first love, Jesus Christ, whose unfailing mercy and love continue to be my heartbeat and an anchor to my soul. Be glorified forever, LORD of Lords. To the precious Holy Spirit, whose guidance continues to be supreme to that of men and women, thank You, Holy Spirit. To my heavenly Father, truly You are the Father of lights and the giver of all good things. Thank You for seeing me fit to share this gift with the world.

Contents

1. Introduction

In a society that often promotes a culture of entitlement and encourages openness, the distinctions between privacy and transparency can frequently become obscured. This book serves as a comprehensive guide, illuminating God-inspired principles that have been utilised by remarkable men and women in the Bible to navigate their lives with intention, wisdom, and purpose.

Within these pages, you'll encounter eight biblical figures whose stories come to life, offering profound insights and lessons on the importance of discretion. These figures include: the courageous Queen Esther, who exemplifies strategic risk-taking; King David, whose journey reflects the complexities of leadership and morality; and Samson, a symbol of strength and vulnerability. You'll also learn from Ruth, whose loyalty and integrity shine through her choices, and the Samaritan Woman at the Well, whose transformative encounter with

Jesus reveals the power of vulnerability and acceptance. Elizabeth, the mother of John the Baptist, offers her insights on faith and fortitude, while Nehemiah, the diligent cup-bearer, demonstrates the significance of purpose-driven action. Finally, our Lord Jesus Christ imparts timeless wisdom that encourages us to reflect inwardly while engaging with a fallen world around us.

This book is a sequel to "The Art of Being Private," building upon its foundations but diving deeper into how these principles can be applied to our lives, particularly in challenging seasons that call for discernment and discretion. Are you prepared to embark on this enriching journey and integrate these powerful lessons into your daily life? As we explore the profound impact of these biblical teachings, my prayer for you is that you may be guided toward discretion, healing, godly wisdom, grace and a purpose-driven existence.

2. Queen Esther

The air in the women's quarters is saturated with the enchanting scents of jasmine, amber, myrrh, honey, saffron, clove and agarwood. Before I indulge in the bathhouse, my maidservants lavish Indian, Ethiopian and Persian oils onto my hair and skin, a ritual to enhance their beauty and health. The wind whispers through the white and blue linen curtains that dress the limestone windows and drape the entranceways as I go about my day. Carvings of warriors and lions embellish the walls, mosaic floors of marble and turquoise, and marble pillars elegantly decorate the ornate garden courts. Exotic fruits, spices, rice dishes with aromatic stews, and meats are readily available, catering to my every whim. They say all that glitters is not gold, but I can assure you that the glittering on these couches, drinking vessels, ceilings, and on my ears, hands, and neck is real gold! My husband, a monarch with a dynasty and an empire spanning from Ethiopia to Asia, is the reason for this opulence. This is my life in the palace as Queen, a life that wasn't always mine, a life I had to earn. I wasn't born with a silver spoon in my mouth!

I was born an orphan and taken under the care of my cousin Mordecai; I didn't always live in the palace until I was brought here (not of my own choice). When I became a queen, those who looked from outside may have envied me and even thought, "here here, she is queen, she has made it, what a rags to riches story!" Perhaps only God knows how hard it was to become who He purposed me to be. My title and role in this kingdom came with actual life-threatening challenges!

Esther 2:7 (NKJV)
And Mordecai had brought up Hadassah, that is, Esther, his uncle's daughter, for she had neither father nor mother. The young woman was lovely and beautiful. When her father and mother died, Mordecai took her as his own daughter.

My name is Hadassah, but many know me as Queen Esther. I am a servant of God's perfect will and design, reflecting a facet of His exceedingly great mercy, favour and compassion. Perhaps, like me, you have been called to be a wife to a husband with a high profile. Maybe you are called into a place of prominence, high influence, net worth or national to international responsibility? For many, being called for such may look like an enviable destiny, but be sober and wise to understand the weight and conditions of walking in and maintaining that call. The bible tells my story, transparently highlighting my challenges along with lessons that I had to learn and apply as a prerequisite to my season's victory. I want to share some of these lessons with you, not to simplify but to acknowledge the complexity of the journey. These lessons will prove to be a sure culmination to walking fully in God's will for you in different seasons of your life.

The Making Of A Wife

Deep within the heart of the Susa, nestled in the very chambers of the palace, a dispute erupted! It was a storm that sought to undermine the masculinity, dignity, and honour of the Monarch, as well as every man in the vast Persian empire. The very foundations of trust and loyalty were shaken as whispers of discontent began to weave their way through the opulent halls. This unexpected turmoil cast a looming shadow of doubt over not only the character of the queen but also the roles and expectations placed upon every wife in the kingdom. It was a moment that demanded scrutiny, as the very essence of their identities seemed at stake. Meanwhile, I found myself oblivious to the brewing chaos. While I was in my cousin's care, engrossed in my usual house duties—preparing meals and managing the household—I was blissfully unaware that this hidden turmoil was about to dramatically alter the course of my life forever.

Esther 1:13-20 (NKJV)

Then the king said to the wise men who understood the times (for this was the king's manner toward all who knew law and justice, those closest to him being Carshena, Shethar, Admatha, Tarshish, Meres, Marsena, and Memucan, the seven princes of Persia and Media, who had access to the king's presence, and who ranked highest in the kingdom): "What shall we do to Queen Vashti, according to law, because she did not obey the command of King Ahasuerus brought to her by the eunuchs?"

And Memucan answered before the king and the princes: "Queen Vashti has not only wronged the king, but also all the princes, and all the people who are in all the provinces of King Ahasuerus. For the queen's behavior will become known to all women, so that they will despise their husbands in their eyes, when they report, 'King Ahasuerus commanded Queen Vashti to be brought in before him, but she did not come.' This very day the noble ladies of Persia and Media will say to all the king's officials that they have heard of the behavior of the queen. Thus there will be excessive contempt and wrath. If it pleases the king, let a royal decree go out from him, and let it be recorded in the laws of the Persians and the Medes, so that it will not be altered, that Vashti shall come no more before King Ahasuerus; and let the king give her royal position to another who is better than she. When the king's decree which he will make is proclaimed throughout all his empire (for it is great), all wives will honor their husbands, both great and small."

Before I was taken to the grand palace, a moment that marked a significant turning point in my life, my cousin Mordecai imparted a crucial piece of advice that would serve as both a foundation and an anchor for me in the coming chapters of my journey. In a world full of potential pitfalls, his words resonated with wisdom and care. Among the many topics a father figure might choose to discuss with his daughter, Mordecai's guidance stood out profoundly: he commanded me to exercise discretion regarding my background and my people! He understood the weight of lineage and that in a place where appearances mattered greatly, it was essential to navigate my identity with utmost privacy.

Mordecai's command to be discreet in the palace was not a request to be pondered on or delayed. It was a directive that demanded immediate and unwavering obedience. In this new and complex environment, the luxury of hesitation, of questioning the motives behind directives, was one I could no longer afford. I understood that in this court ruled by power and prestige, my ability to obey without falter was not just a sign of loyalty but a crucial survival strategy for navigating the intricacies of royal life. The lessons I had learned in Mordecai's modest dwelling were about to be tested and expanded upon in ways I had never imagined possible.

Esther 2:10 (NKJV)
Esther had not revealed her people or family, for Mordecai had charged her not to reveal it.

[Hebrew word for revealed is nāḡaḏ which means to declare, tell, utter, certify, profess, manifest, fully, denounce, expound]
[Hebrew word for charged is ṣāvâ which means to command, forbid,]

Throughout my life, I have come to appreciate the profound strength found in humility, a lesson I learned from the unwavering guidance of Mordecai. He wasn't just my guardian; he embodied both the nurturing roles of a father and a mother, instilling in me a set of values that would shape my character. Under his watchful eye, I honed the art of listening—truly absorbing rather than merely hearing—along with the practice of obeying without questioning the wisdom behind his directives.

These traits were often birthed out of pressure, quiet seasons and low moments. Little did I realise that these very traits, cultivated in the simplicity of our daily life, would prove essential as I transitioned to a completely different existence within the ornate walls of a palace.

So, when this new season came, it required greater humility. I could not have anticipated that my very survival in this grand, unfamiliar realm would depend intensely on my capacity to listen attentively, learn diligently, and follow the meticulous instructions set forth by Hegai, who was appointed as the keeper of all the virgin maidens destined for the king's attention, in a vast Persian empire.

Esther 2:8-9 (NKJV)

So it was, when the king's command and decree were heard, and when many young women were gathered at Shushan the citadel, under the custody of Hegai, that Esther also was taken to the king's palace, into the care of Hegai the custodian of the women. Now the young woman pleased him, and she obtained his favor; so he readily gave beauty preparations to her, besides her allowance. Then seven choice maidservants were provided for her from the king's palace, and he moved her and her maidservants to the best place in the house of the women.

In a society like today's, which has liberated opinions and views of what misogyny and feminism look like, how would one who has a similar calling like mine take orders, commands and instructions from the opposite sex, especially one they radically despise or don't respect?

The world vainly values strength that is exhibited through possessions and titles, often missing the concealed strength hidden in good character and how well one treats others. The point is, how many men and women have forfeited their purpose, inheritance, and calling due to misconceptions about what weakness or strength looks like? How can we forget that the value of character is immeasurable and that it can lead to success and fulfilment beyond what external strength and possessions can offer?

When the other maidens and I were under the custody of Hegai, I won his favour amongst all the maidens not because of my good looks but because of my conduct and character. Beloved, pure discretion is deeper than keeping secrets and being quiet; it ought to flow from a place of meaning, your character through humility, willingness to learn, and being teachable and obedient to your calling. If I could submit under and win my custodian's favour, indeed, I could also submit under and obtain my future husband's favour, the king. Reflect on the importance of humility, willingness to learn, and obedience in your relationships.

The Making Of A Queen

Before my ascension to the throne, I endured a gruelling 12-month training regimen involving the application of oils and perfumes to my body and skin. While many are captivated by the allure of this training, the reality is far from glamorous. The process was fraught with pain, pressure, tears of frustration, lingering demotivation, and profound loneliness—all hidden beneath the sweet scent of the perfumes and the rejuvenating effects of the oils.

For the first 6 months, oil of Myrrh was administered to us. It was extracted by wounding a tree through its bark into the sapwood to secrete and bleed out the myrrh resin. It is no wonder why Myrrh prophetically symbolised the sufferings of the Son of God, Jesus Christ, for the world's redemption and salvation. For us maidens, however, the oil held a different kind of redemption—one that attended to our natural beauty by addressing skin imperfections. The oil of Myrrh worked wonders! It healed our wounds, sunburns, scars, wrinkles, blemishes, cracks, stretch marks, rashes and many skin diseases; restoring health. The oil was thick and rich with vibrant shades of brown, yellow and amber, embalmed in bitter but captivating aromas. It was powerful enough to penetrate right through the skin epidermis.

For the latter half of the training, Hegai introduced a new phase. The beauty treatments shifted from the oil of Myrrh to perfumes and sweet aromas, heralding a new chapter in our training, one that would purify and polish our skin.

Esther 2:12 (NKJV)

Each young woman's turn came to go in to King Ahasuerus after she had completed twelve months' preparation, according to the regulations for the women, for thus were the days of their preparation apportioned: six months with oil of myrrh, and six months with perfumes and preparations for beautifying women.

Many imagine being drenched, massaged, and rubbed with oils and perfumes for 12 months to be enjoyable and relaxing! However, reality proved to be quite different when the other maidens and I underwent this process. It demanded extraordinary transparency from each of us, pushing us far beyond mere physical undressing. We were called to strip away the layers of our garments, exposing not only our skin but also our innermost emotions and vulnerabilities, as our skin, hair, and bodies were being assessed, judged, and prepared for purification. Letting go of the shame of our bodies, scars and bruises and being willing to be examined under the careful eyes of our administrators.

The massages and treatments were not merely relaxing; they often included moments of discomfort. There were instances when the application of the oils was accompanied by vigorous poking and pinching, intended to stimulate circulation between the skin and oils for maximising healing. On certain days, the treatments were particularly painful, especially when unwanted hairs were removed, and the skin was primed for purification. During these 12 months of treatments, the maidens, who were spoilt and accustomed to making tantrums, did not win any favours with Hegai, but rather, they became like thorns in his eyes.

Beloved, at some point, you will also go through this same training on your road to purpose! Perhaps in a different setting, however, the essence remains unchanged: pressure will be applied during those seasons, forcing you to confront and let go of traits like pride, impatience, and a desire for control. It is during these times that the true character of your heart will be revealed, often stripping away your facade. Moreover, it won't be enjoyable to discover parts of you that don't look, smell or feel (touch) presentable according to God's standard for your assignment. Parts of you need to be worked on and healed to strengthen you in your God-given assignment. You will quickly learn that impatience, tantrums, control, and manipulation will not improve your progress but delay it. That growth in the face of discomfort leads to the maturity necessary for fulfilling your divinely appointed purpose.

As my days in the vast and opulent palace unfolded, so too did the weight of my mounting responsibilities, each day becoming heavier than the last. I bore the considerable burden of safeguarding my true identity, people, and nation. While the other women in the palace freely shared their childhood stories and laughed together in the women's courts, I remained silent, bound by the duty of being discreet and private.

The memories of my own childhood were marked with pain; I had lost both my father and mother. Yet even in the midst of that sorrow, I felt I did not have the liberty or the safe space to share my story—the story of my losses and struggles. Also, living with other beautiful women would require me to be drama-free, friendly and kind, given that I couldn't reveal my family and identity. Moreover, this effort to keep my identity veiled was not without its sacrifices; it meant I had to compromise on some of my Jewish dietary laws and customs, adopting the mannerisms and even the attire of a Persian woman. I understood this was part of my larger mission to protect my people and the nation I held dear.

Beloved, there are seasons of our lives where we will not have the liberty to speak up, defend ourselves or even glory in our private victories. This is because such seasons demand discretion to preserve you for the next season of God's plan for you. However, this is a revelation you will need to receive directly from God concerning the value of your next season; only then will you find the understanding to cooperate fully with God's purpose! It will not be easy to keep your mouth shut, your emotions under subjection, and your posture aligned to the direction of God's purpose, but eventually, your faithfulness and humility to obey God through discretion will reap a harvest of victory and preparation!

Nevertheless, my living conditions were upgraded after I obtained Hegai's favour. In recognition of my potential and worth, I was appointed seven skilled and intelligent women who would attend to my needs, assisting me as I navigated the complexities of life within the palace walls. In moments like these, I marvelled at how God had a unique way of easing our burdens and providing for our needs.

For me, the move to another part of the palace represented far more than just a shift towards luxury or comfort; it was about focus and purpose. The change of residence meant I could concentrate on being moulded into a Queen through the 12-month treatments we undertook. God knew that these months of purification required my full attention instead of worrying if I was behaving Persian enough in front of others or if I was allowing my guard to slip when questions regarding my identity arose.

Esther 2:13-14 (NKJV)
Thus prepared, each young woman went to the king, and she was given whatever she desired to take with her from the women's quarters to the king's palace. In the evening she went, and in the morning she returned to the second house of the women, to the custody of Shaashgaz, the king's eunuch who kept the concubines. She would not go in to the king again unless the king delighted in her and called for her by name.

After an entire year dedicated to the rigorous process of purification, the moment had finally arrived for me to present myself to the king. While many might have chosen to embellish themselves with exquisite jewels or fineries sourced from the lavish collections of the palace, I made a different choice. Hagai taught me that true beauty and worth do not stem from outward appearances but from the richness of the spirit and the depth of one's character. I adorned myself not with opulent decorations but with the profound wisdom and knowledge that Hegai generously shared with me during my time of preparation. My true adornment was not external but internal, reflecting my trust and submission. This choice and decision not only earned me favour with Hegai but also with all who saw me.

Esther 2:16 -17 NKJV

So Esther was taken to King Ahasuerus, into his royal palace, in the tenth month, which is the month of Tebeth, in the seventh year of his reign. The king loved Esther more than all the other women, and she obtained grace and favor in his sight more than all the virgins; so he set the royal crown upon her head and made her queen instead of Vashti.

Favour In The Midst Of Discretion

In this moment of joyous celebration, complete bliss, and satisfaction, I would have never foreseen the quiet storm brewing inside the heart of one of the king's most esteemed princes, Haman. A storm within these very palace walls aimed at eradicating the entire Jewish population scattered across all the king's provinces. This insidious scheme, wielded by someone so close to the throne, threatened to unravel my reign right under my nose!

Esther 3:13 -14 (NKJV)

And the letters were sent by couriers into all the king's provinces, to destroy, to kill, and to annihilate all the Jews, both young and old, little children and women, in one day, on the thirteenth day of the twelfth month, which is the month of Adar, and to plunder their possessions. A copy of the document was to be issued as law in every province, being published for all people, that they should be ready for that day. The couriers went out, hastened by the king's command; and the decree was proclaimed in Shushan the citadel. So the king and Haman sat down to drink, but the city of Shushan was perplexed.

Mordecai has always been a figure of remarkable strength and unwavering resilience; his ability to endure hardship without revealing a hint of vulnerability has been one of his most admirable traits. So, when I discovered that he was openly weeping in the city, clad in sackcloth and ashes, it struck me with a profound sense of alarm! This sight was so foreign to his usual demeanour that it deeply unsettled me.

Before I ascended to the throne as Queen, I had the privilege of being mentored by Hegai, whose wisdom and guidance paved the way for my rise to power. Now, as I sat in the palace, a position both coveted and burdening, I found myself grappling with a delicate dilemma: could I still seek Hegai's counsel for issues that were entirely separate from the king or my royal responsibilities? I was now Queen, and I had to think like one, yet I also had to maintain my secret identity as Mordecai's cousin, a Jew.

In that moment of uncertainty, my heart ached for Mordecai. I longed to reach out to him, to wrap my arms around him, to wipe away the tears that stained his cheeks, and to offer reassurance that the turmoil he was

experiencing would eventually resolve itself for the better.

I sent garments of linen and silk with precious embroidery

to calm and clothe him while also symbolising hope for a

brighter future and, more so, to remove the filthy

sackcloths.

Esther 4:13-14 (NKJV)
And Mordecai told them to answer Esther: "Do not think in
your heart that you will escape in the king's palace any more
than all the other Jews. For if you remain completely silent at
this time, relief and deliverance will arise for the Jews from
another place, but you and your father's house will perish. Yet
who knows whether you have come to the kingdom for such a
time as this?"

Upon reflection on Mordecai's stern words, it was

clear that I had not understood the complete perplexity of

my cousin's mourning. At first, I failed to grasp the

magnitude of the calamity that loomed over us. It was a

threat that could not be swept under the rug of soft, new,

expensive clothes and sweet words of comfort. The

sackcloth he wore was made out of black goat's hair, the

fabric rough against his skin, a deliberate choice symbolising mourning. The ashes upon his head were not based on a personal issue but symbolic of holy repentance for the grievous affliction that had come upon our people. There was great mourning among many of my people in all the king's provinces! So much so that it finally dawned on me that though I had kept my nationality and identity private throughout my stay and promotion in the palace, my "revered" title of 5 years as Queen was not enough to secure my life as a Jew!

Beloved, have you ever found yourself placing too much trust in your position, title, or wealth only to be blindsided by a crisis that could sweep it all away? Your crisis may not mirror mine, but it could be an economic or health crisis. As it is written, 'Some trust in their war chariots and others in their horses, but we trust in the power of the LORD our God.' In our most vulnerable moments, we can turn to the all-powerful God, whose grace, wisdom, and mercy can replenish, restore, and sustain us.

Esther 4:15-16 (NKJV)
Then Esther told them to reply to Mordecai: "Go, gather all the Jews who are present in Shushan, and fast for me; neither eat nor drink for three days, night or day. My maids and I will fast likewise. And so I will go to the king, which is against the law; and if I perish, I perish!"

In the quiet confines of my chambers, I sought the favour of my loyal maidens, who were unaware of my Jewish heritage but placed their trust in me for a shared cause. They willingly joined me on this mission to fast for 3 days and 3 nights. We abstained not only from food and drink but also from our royal comforts, shedding our ornate garments and fragrant perfumes. In the seclusion of my chambers, we gathered, united in both our tears and fervent prayers, calling upon God's boundless mercies, clinging to the hope that our sacrifices would be received. May you, beloved, also find companions who will uplift and not hinder your spiritual journey!

As the days of fasting drew to a close, a sense of anticipation filled the air. I prepared for the momentous encounter, adorning myself with perfume and wearing my finest royal robe, ensuring that I presented myself as fitting for the occasion. The time had come for me to step into my destiny, and I was ready.

Esther 5:2-3 (NKJV)
So it was, when the king saw Queen Esther standing in the court, that she found favor in his sight, and the king held out to Esther the golden scepter that was in his hand. Then Esther went near and touched the top of the scepter. And the king said to her, "What do you wish, Queen Esther? What is your request? It shall be given to you—up to half the kingdom!"

When I found favour in the king's sight, he would grant me up to half his kingdom. In that pivotal moment, it dawned on me that the time for maintaining my secret was at an end. Beloved, do you realise that discretion is not a permanent garment; it has an expiration date that only your season can illuminate? It is written, 'There's a time for every purpose under the heavens, a time to gain, and a time to lose; a time to keep, and a time to throw away.'

I now needed to disclose my true self to the king to save my people. Yet, without knowing whether the king would hear my plea and grant me favour again, my heart was filled with profound wisdom that could only have been from God. I felt a profound sense of wisdom wash over me, one that could only have been bestowed by God Himself. I requested not my deliverance but a banquet of wine to honour the king and Haman, the enemy of the Jews. The king, known for his enjoyment of grand feasts and indulgent libations, would indeed find delight in such a celebration. However, in an extraordinary twist of fate, a lavish banquet, which once brought about the downfall of Queen Vashti, would serve as the very platform for my own salvation and eternal security within the king's realm.

At the second banquet, orchestrated through God's divine guidance, I prepared to make the ultimate sacrifice. With my heart racing and courage igniting my spirit, I spoke up before the king and Haman, bracing myself for what was to come. In that critical instant, I revealed my true identity—the essence of who I was, the most precious possession I held. With words that felt as if they were etched upon my soul by God's hand, I petitioned the king not just for my life but for the lives of my people as well. At that moment, the coin flipped, the season changed, and my true deliverance no longer came from hiding but from the courage to reveal myself.

Esther 7:3-6 (NKJV)

Then Queen Esther answered and said, "If I have found favor in your sight, O king, and if it pleases the king, let my life be given me at my petition, and my people at my request. For we have been sold, my people and I, to be destroyed, to be killed, and to be annihilated. Had we been sold as male and female slaves, I would have held my tongue, although the enemy could never compensate for the king's loss." So King Ahasuerus answered and said to Queen Esther, "Who is he, and where is he, who would dare presume in his heart to do such a thing?" And Esther said, "The adversary and enemy is this wicked Haman!"So Haman was terrified before the king and queen.

When the enemy of people, Haman, was exposed, he was immediately put to death on the gallows he had premeditated to hang Mordecai! Had I abandoned discretion and revealed my people and identity any sooner than that moment at the banquet, I can't say I would have still been queen, let alone alive. The stark reality of knowing when to speak and when to be silent played an integral part in the deliverance of the entire nation of the Jews throughout all the provinces of the king's kingdom. Beloved, have you considered the potential costs of lacking discretion in your own life? It could be a generation, an honourable career, children, marriage, or ministry. It might set you back in immeasurable ways! The choice to exercise caution and wisdom can shape not just your destiny but the destinies of others.

Prayer

Heavenly Father, you know my end from my beginning. I may not fully understand the seasons of my life, but by Your grace, I know You will never leave me nor forsake me. You will walk with me through them. In this season of my life, if discretion is required, I pray for the capacity to be discreet to fulfil the mission you have birthed in me. As You did with Esther, give me wisdom to navigate this season with ease and strength. Teach me to know when to disclose things and when to conceal things. In Jesus' name, I pray, amen.

3. The Samaritan Woman At The Well

Discretion, often associated with privacy, was more than that for me. It was a way of navigating the world around me—a choice I was forced to make. My discretion was a veil of secrecy I wore for a significant part of my life. I was living in the grip of shame, my choices and decisions a constant echo of life's harshness. The consequences of the tangled web of my romantic endeavours were a burden of shame I carried, a weight that seemed to grow heavier with each passing day. The struggle to maintain my discretion often left me feeling trapped, yearning for the freedom to express myself without fear of judgment or reproach.

Far From A Fairytale

As I gaze into the mirror, my flaws seem to mock me. More lines etched on my once flawless skin. The weight of deceit, concealment, and pretence in my life is beginning to show. Notwithstanding the desire of longing for a loving husband, a provider who cherishes me not just for my outward beauty but for the commitment of marriage. I crave the warmth of family dinners and the joy of shared laughter. I yearn for a family of my own, but that dream seems to slip further away with each passing day.

These thoughts were my morning routine, a daily escape from the reality of a life I yearned for, a life I believed I should have been brought up to. With a sigh, I hastily wrap my shawl around my hair, eager to embark on my journey into the hot valley to Jacob's well. You see, Sychar is a hot country, and the well that Jacob gave us in his time continued to be a valuable asset.

Now, customarily, women did not come during midday to draw out water from the well; they went in the evening when it was cooler, but not so for me. I had to time my journey around noon, though, at this time, the sun was at its peak. Yet, the scorching heat afforded me freedom from ridicule, jeering, sneering, and insults from those who knew my past and present. So then, unlike most, who could stay sheltered in their homes, I had to face the intensity of the sun at noonday to draw water, all to avoid people.

Moreover, in the midst of all this, there was a stark cultural divide between Jews and Samaritans, and I found myself on the fringes, struggling to find my place. The exclusions were clear, and I was left to fend for myself, battling against the societal norms that sought to keep us apart, along with my own marital woes. All these factors snared me into a corner of being discreet towards who I could interact with, where I could go, and even what time of day I could be seen in public.

Also, my many sins of immorality and way of life disqualified me from society's rigid expectations of young women, casting me as an outcast. These 'sins' were often the result of circumstances beyond my control. Still, society was quick to judge and condemn, leaving me isolated and alone. Besides trying as much as I could to be discreet, it was hard for me to fit in with both the Jewish and Samaritan virgins. Their conversations, laughter, and shared experiences felt like a distant world I could never be a part of. Over time, self-pity, rejection, and shame had taken over me. I felt like an outsider, unworthy of their company. Let me elaborate! You see, drawing water, a task typically undertaken by young women, was more than a mere thirst-quencher. It was a covert audition for marriage, a chance to attract a potential suitor! Do not assume that the Jewish virgins were unaware of the fairytale-like story of their ancestors, Rebecca and Jacob, who first met at a well.

Genesis 29:10-11 (NKJV)

And it came to pass, when Jacob saw Rachel the daughter of Laban his mother's brother, and the sheep of Laban his mother's brother, that Jacob went near and rolled the stone from the well's mouth, and watered the flock of Laban his mother's brother. Now while he was still speaking with them, Rachel came with her father's sheep, for she was a shepherdess. Then Jacob kissed Rachel, and lifted up his voice and wept.

This is "the" well of Jacob and virgins who came here also hoped to meet their future husband! Indeed, going to the well was steeped in cultural significance, and it also meant that women were vetted out from a distance. For instance, status was often shown through the number and quality of livestock one owned, indicating a family's wealth and ability to provide. Moreover, titles were associated with one's household name and offered insight into a family's reputation and standing within the community. Beauty, too, was assessed based on clothing and appearance. These cultural norms, whether one was Jewish or Samaritan, played a significant role when we women went to the well with or without flocks to water. This was more than just about getting vessels filled with water; it intertwined a woman's daily responsibilities with the quest for future security and commitment! Being an outcast, as I often felt, set me back from securing commitment and a future in a way that the Jewish virgins could. They seemed to navigate this social landscape with ease and confidence due to their established reputations.

Beloved, perhaps you are in a place of setback like I was? Perhaps it's not in the area of marriage, but when you compare yourself with others, do you feel a deep sense of hopelessness and despair?

As I went to draw water, I carried a tough exterior, seemingly resilient even when no one important was around. Yet, inside, I was burdened by the weight of cultural rejection and societal shame. Little did I know that this day would be different. This was the day I would have an unexpected encounter with a Man named Jesus, who would empower a woman like me and rewrite my life and love story, transforming my despair into hope!

The Gift

As I was engrossed in the mundane task of drawing water, I found myself trying to hide the myriad of emotions which my eyes failed to not reflect. Suddenly, a Man called out to me in the most gentle voice, "Give Me a drink." In that moment, I shifted my focus from the water I depended on and the memories of my five failed marriages, to this enigmatic figure before me. He was devoid of any desirable beauty or comeliness, yet He radiated a compelling presence that drew my attention to Him.

As the heat of the day had intensified, I was more taken aback by the unexpected nature of this situation. His accent and attire clearly identified him as a Jew. Yet, here He was, openly conversing with me, a Samaritan woman. The sweltering heat only added to the surreal nature of this moment. Unless you lived under a rock, it was clear that the tension between our cultures was palpable, with Jews typically holding a deep disdain for us Samaritans. It was a genuinely astonishing encounter in a world bound by norms. I couldn't believe that this Man would defy such deeply ingrained gender inequality and cultural exclusions just to quench His thirst with water from me!

Perhaps, like me, in that moment, Jesus is also trying to divert your gaze from your problems and woes. Could it be that He is compelling you today to fix your eyes on His face today? Is He challenging you to relinquish something because you have outgrown it and need to move on to something better, maybe even because you simply deserve better?

In our society of gender inequality, women were often seen as burdens to society. A perception that dates back to the days of Adam and Eve in the Garden of Eden, where a woman was held responsible for the downfall of mankind by many. Sadly, women continue to face the consequences of this historical narrative, even though God held both the man and woman, Adam and Eve, accountable for their wrongdoings. These are deeply ingrained inconsistencies in our society. Nevertheless, amid these norms, I found it remarkable that Jesus did not

conform, by asking me for a drink.

John 4:9-10 (NKJV)
Then the woman of Samaria said to Him, "How is it that You,
being a Jew, ask a drink from me, a Samaritan woman?" For
Jews have no dealings with Samaritans. Jesus answered and
said to her, "If you knew the gift of God, and who it is who says
to you, 'Give Me a drink,' you would have asked Him, and He
would have given you living water."

He was unlike any other Jewish man, transcending

tradition, and openly challenging cultural, racial, and

gender divisions. However, in that unique moment, I

couldn't fully comprehend the depth of His limitless grace.

But I would soon discover that I could live in a realm of

unimaginable fulfilment, where I would no longer have to

rely on a well for water; a temporary solution to my

problems. Indeed, the truth is that though I needed

solutions and answers to my marital and love woes, what I

really needed was the gift of God, eternal life in Him who

never leaves nor forsakes us, unlike my previous 5 husbands, who I couldn't keep.

If I had known I was in the presence of the Creator of all things, I would have asked for all of Him, for He is the living One! With Him is the permanent procurement - the promised Holy Spirit, the seal of redemption and life. Furthermore, the Holy Spirit is living water; baptising every area of one's heart and saturating the soul and spirit from all spiritual thirst! I was in the company of the ultimate fulfilment and giver of life.

What Jesus was offering me, the well could not sustain! Unfortunately, I hadn't yet perceived that truth, so I measured God's living water using human resources. I looked at Jesus and concluded that He lacked the tools to give me this living water. How, when and where can He fulfil this great thing He speaks of? My understanding was limited to cups, pitchers and buckets. I failed to realise that Jesus' love is all-encompassing, capable of addressing all aspects of my life and providing refreshment.

It is entirely possible to encounter God but not experience His power, miracles or presence because He doesn't look, sound or speak in a way that is familiar to you.

John 4:11-12 (AMP)
She said to Him, "Sir, You have nothing to draw with [no bucket and rope] and the well is deep. Where then do You get that living water? Are You greater than our father Jacob, who gave us the well, and who used to drink from it himself, and his sons and his cattle also?"

Beloved, are you limiting your understanding of the true essence of your life on earth because your insight and revelation of where you should be is limited to physical elements? Do you know that God's power and grace encompass life beyond the physical elements that look like solutions to your problems.

Even with my attention on Jesus, I still lacked the capacity to see myself the way He saw me! He saw me liberated from thirst a vision I couldn't fully grasp. With

your attention on Jesus, can you reach your hand of faith
to His? Can your eyes be open to living in the freedom
God has freely given you? This freedom transcends
tradition, trends, religion and the systems of the world.

Here I was, blindly reiterating Jacob's greatness to
Jacob's potter. I didn't recognise the living embodiment of
God's Word standing before me was He who had created
and formed Jacob. To me, my people and the Jews, Jacobs
well was a source of hope in our day-to-day life. Yet, it is a
fleeting hope. The giver of hope was here! Jesus is greater
than Jacob, who gave that well! I thought, as long as we
have the well of Jacob, at least we have some kind of
posterity because he, his children and his livestock drank
from it! How fleeting is the posterity of the earth in
comparison to life in Jesus? Our careers and jobs are
fleeting. Our financial safety nets are fleeting; even life
itself is fleeting; all have no eternal life and will become
dust. There is, however, a heavenly posterity that will last
forever and is eternal through Jesus Christ. I adorned my
identity with the fleeting posterity of my father Jacob. Yet,

at that very moment, I was speaking with He who is the Way, Truth and Life. He was the gate to eternal posterity.

Beloved, are you still viewing the move of God from an old lens like I did? Are you looking at physical wells but out of your belly is an overflow of living waters. Are you able to see that God has begun a new thing in this era and you need to see from the perspective of the Holy Spirit?

John 4:13-14 (NKJV)

Jesus answered and said to her, "Whoever drinks of this water will thirst again, but whoever drinks of the water that I shall give him will never thirst. But the water that I shall give him will become in him a fountain of water springing up into everlasting life."

The water found at the well of Jacob, while refreshing to the body, falls short of reaching the deeper issues of the soul. In a moment of reflection, I realised that my soul was in turmoil, weighed down by various burdens that were manifestations of my inner struggles. Though I was physically present, my heart was a living testament to the troubles that plagued me, and I felt an intense longing to quench a deeper thirst—one that transcends mere physical needs. The water from the well may relieve temporary dryness in the mouth, but it fails to soothe the persistent cravings of the spirit.

This realisation struck me: the conventional waters of this world might address our bodily needs, but they are powerless against the shortfalls that affect our spirit and soul. Only living water could address and penetrate into the issues in my soul. His living water was the active presence of God and His Word in a submitted heart. Only then could I be delivered from my life of discretion chained to shame and self-pity bound in my heart.

Beloved, are you consistently turning to sources that merely relieve the dryness of your physical needs while neglecting the deeper thirst of your soul? With the Holy Spirit, God wants you to become a fountain, watering others with nourishment that holds eternal significance enriched by the gifts and fruits of the Holy Spirit. Whoever receives the Holy Spirit will never thirst again, for out of them flows rivers of living water. Out of them is a source of sustenance that changes lives around them and in them. Not only do they become a well, but they also grow into rivers!

Discretion Anchored In Truth

John 4:16-18 NKJV
Jesus said to her, "Go, call your husband, and come here." The woman answered and said, "I have no husband." Jesus said to her, "You have well said, 'I have no husband,' for you have had five husbands, and the one whom you now have is not your husband; in that you spoke truly."

The truth that I had been hiding and ashamed to whisper even to the most unassuming of people in this town. Yet, there was something about the presence of Jesus that compelled me to lay bare the secrets of my heart, peeling back the layers of pretence I had so carefully constructed. As I stood there, the weight of my hidden struggles began to lift, and I found myself pouring out my truth in an act of submission that felt both terrifying and liberating.

They often say that it is easier to share your deepest secrets with a stranger; perhaps that held some truth in my case. The heat of the day was intense, but it paled in comparison to the warmth of protection and hope that radiated from Jesus. In that moment, I felt an unmistakable urge to be authentic, to embrace

vulnerability, and to step away from the shadows of

inauspiciousness I had clung to for so long. The number 5

is often associated with grace, but when it came to me, I

had failed 5 times! The man who now stood at the centre

of my affections, I was not yet committed to.

John 4:19-20 (NKJV)
The woman said to Him, "Sir, I perceive that You are a
prophet. Our fathers worshiped on this mountain, and you Jews
say that in Jerusalem is the place where one ought to worship."

Still reserved and leaning on the stick of discretion

anchoring my soul through shame, I was reluctant to let

the feelings he ignited in me burrow deeper, fearful of

exposing the deeply rooted trauma of rejection and shame

I had accumulated over the years. Bitterness had woven its

threads through the fabric of my heart, and I was uncertain

if I was ready to confront it head-on. So, I set my heart to

explore His prophetic insight. I began to question the

very foundations of my core beliefs. Could it be that all

my decisions, choices, and the misfortune I endured were rooted in a place of misguided worship?

In the midst of deliverance, God values the effort we put in through transparency. By humbling myself before Him, I opened my heart and mind, allowing my eyes to fully perceive the magnificence of His true identity. I realised that He is indeed the Christ—the embodiment of hope and salvation. In trying to find out the controversial truth about the true essence of worship, I found myself embarking on a spiritual exploration that surpassed my expectations. Instead of merely uncovering theoretical knowledge about worship, I discovered Someone far more significant. I encountered Jesus the Christ!

John 4:21-30, 39 (NKJV)

Jesus said to her, "Woman, believe Me, the hour is coming when you will neither on this mountain, nor in Jerusalem, worship the Father. You worship what you do not know; we know what we worship, for salvation is of the Jews. But the hour is coming, and now is, when the true worshipers will worship the Father in spirit and truth; for the Father is seeking such to worship Him. God is Spirit, and those who worship Him must worship in spirit and truth." The woman said to Him, "I know that Messiah is coming" (who is called Christ). "When He comes, He will tell us all things."Jesus said to her, "I who speak to you am He." And at this point His disciples came, and they marveled that He talked with a woman; yet no one said, "What do You seek?" or, "Why are You talking with her?" The woman then left her water-pot, went her way into the city, and said to the men, "Come, see a Man who told me all things that I ever did. Could this be the Christ?" Then they went out of the city and came to Him… And many of the Samaritans of that city believed in Him because of the word of the woman who testified, "He told me all that I ever did."

Beloved, Jesus Christ is waiting for you to discover His true identity, and this discovery begins with aligning your worship with Him. Perhaps you have worshipped your pain, misfortune, spouse, family or possessions? These earthly things are fleeting and do not endure. In contrast, the life found in Christ and the love He offers are eternal treasures that cannot be taken away.

When I first encountered Christ, it felt as though a radiant light pierced through the dark corners of my heart, areas filled with shame, guilt, and emotional pain. I realised that I no longer had to live my life in secrecy or allow my past to dictate my future. What I once perceived as necessary discretion—hiding my struggles and vulnerabilities—was actually rooted in a deep-seated shame that kept me chained. However, knowing that Jesus Christ was present and intimately aware of my struggles allowed me to embrace my true identity as a beloved child of God. The truth being that I was acquainted with God and He was here in the flesh! My deepest secrets no longer carried shame but now carried the brilliance of God's ever-unfailing presence. God sees me! I am enough, I am loved, and I am free! I believed in the Messiah, Jesus Christ.

Jesus was sent to the lost sheep of Israel, yet I, being part-Gentile, was engrafted in God's master plan of salvation. As it is written, "for God so loved the world..." Jesus, in His profound compassion, took the time to divert His journey because He needed to go through Samaria and reach out to me, one society overlooked. This alone highlights God's perfect and inclusive plan for humanity. This Jesus—full of love and grace—makes a priority of those who often find themselves marginalised or overlooked by others. He, the only Begotten Son of God, met me, an outsider yearning for belonging.

Likewise, He can meet you right where you are today because God has time for you too. Perhaps you need a true personal encounter with Jesus that will bring out your authenticity and vulnerability? I'm confident that as You yield your heart to His, that encounter will soon come and completely change how you see yourself to seeing and walking in wholeness, even if things are imperfect.

Prayer

Heavenly Father, shame, guilt and fear have backed me into a corner of discretion. Hiding and pretending have become a way of life because of heartbreak and disappointments. I pray for a genuine encounter with Your Son, Jesus Christ, and to walk in the deliverance and wholeness of His finished work on the Cross. I pray that by Your Holy Spirit, You teach me to apply discretion from a place of authenticity, joy and peace. In the name of Jesus, I pray, amen.

4. King David

Despise Not Small Beginnings

Baa…baa… was the bleating sound of my audience joining me in worship as I joyfully sang songs to God, the Creator of the heavens, the earth and everything in them. This expansive field of Bethlehem bathed in the golden light of dawn, became my sacred sanctuary. The gentle whisper of the wind wove itself through the melodies I sang, creating a heavenly harmony that enveloped us. As the first rays of sunlight illuminated the valley, the long shadows cast by the ancient trees appeared to sway in time with the rhythm of my praise, a breathtaking display of nature joining me in worship. My spirit soared as I sang songs to my Maker, revelling in the pure act of worship.

Moreover, this morning was a triumph! The sheep had remained nestled within our little flock, none had strayed from the fold, and the areas surrounding us were void of any lurking serpents or wild beasts threatening our peace. With a heart full of anticipation for the adventures that lay ahead, I leaped joyfully, spinning in circles filled with gratitude for the gift of a new day filled with new mercies.

Throughout my time as a young shepherd, I learned to cultivate my own brand of joy, often through creativity and imagination. I often found solace in playing my delicate harp while my flock grazed peacefully around me. At times, I couldn't help but break into spontaneous psalms of praise.

1 Samuel 17:13-15 (NKJV)
The three oldest sons of Jesse had gone to follow Saul to the battle. The names of his three sons who went to the battle were Eliab the firstborn, next to him Abinadab, and the third Shammah. David was the youngest. And the three oldest followed Saul. But David occasionally went and returned from Saul to feed his father's sheep at Bethlehem.

As the caretaker of my father's flock, I often found myself spending long days and sleepless nights tending to the sheep. Some of my brothers had forfeited the privilege of caring for our father's sheep by joining King Saul to go to war. I call it a privilege, yet you might wonder what I gained from spending all that time in the fields rather than donning armour alongside my brothers? However, for me, the sense of duty drove my commitment.

This sense of responsibility is often overlooked by those caught up in the glories of the battlefield. Yet, that sense of duty pivots one into the path of purpose. In the quiet moments of watching over the flock, ensuring their safety and well-being, I learned the value of leadership, patience and dedication. There were countless hours when it felt like my efforts were futile, as if I were standing still while others raced toward fame and fortune. But I held onto my faith and believed my diligence would yield fruit. During those humble moments, filled with labour and a sense of accomplishment, I began to understand my purpose. After all, these humble beginnings, though they seemed mundane, forged my character and shaped my mind for the greater challenges that lay ahead.

These lessons learned in the fields—the importance of stewardship, the strength found in perseverance, and the humility that comes from serving—were all vital preparations when I ascended to the throne. As I tended and fed my father's flock, my love for each sheep grew deeper. Their safety, welfare, and health became of utmost priority. I studied and recognised each one, ensuring that none would be lost under my watch. Though I was a steward for my father, the sheep became mine, and I became theirs, for they knew my voice.

No thrill of war, silver armour, or battle songs could diminish my care for these sheep. I had tasted life in the palace when I played the lyre for King Saul, but my duty as a shepherd kept me back. It was a sacrifice I embraced, a choice I made willingly because my love and commitment to my flock were unmatched. I chose the humble path of a shepherd over the glories of the palace.

David! David! A voice called out, abruptly stopping the flow of my praise session. From a distance, as soft rays of morning light peered, touching the long grass, the scent of the morning dew mingling with the earthy smell of the flock. I saw a faint silhouette shuffling towards me as if weighed down. As the figure approached nearer, I soon realised that my father was coming towards me with items in his hands.

1 Samuel 17:17-20 (NKJV)

Then Jesse said to his son David, "Take now for your brothers an ephah of this dried grain and these ten loaves, and run to your brothers at the camp. And carry these ten cheeses to the captain of their thousand, and see how your brothers fare, and bring back news of them." Now Saul and they and all the men of Israel were in the Valley of Elah, fighting with the Philistines. So David rose early in the morning, left the sheep with a keeper, and took the things and went as Jesse had commanded him. And he came to the camp as the army was going out to the fight and shouting for the battle.

Even Champions Can Fall

As I made my way to the camp of Israel, the anticipation of seeing my brothers soon changed into a sense of unease as I took in the scene before me. There they were, the armies of Israel ranged up for battle in the vivid green rolling hills surrounding the Valley of Elah. Yet, terror and anguish gripped their hearts, their strength fragile as a reed in the sea. The silence that enveloped the camp was unsettling, broken only by the whispering wind that carried the heavy weight of dread with it. In the distance, the Philistine forces loomed, their confidence radiating with every echo of their leader's commanding voice. Towering nearly three meters tall, he was meticulously furnished in awe-striking armour, which looked like pieces of art. His presence was magnified by the strange beauty of his weapons. One of his weapons, a spear, was extraordinary, having a head thick like a weaver's beam! He came forward speaking boisterous words against the armies of Israel.

1 Samuel 17:4-7 (NKJV)
And a champion went out from the camp of the Philistines,
named Goliath, from Gath, whose height was six cubits and a
span. He had a bronze helmet on his head, and he was armed
with a coat of mail, and the weight of the coat was five
thousand shekels of bronze. And he had bronze armor on his
legs and a bronze javelin between his shoulders. Now the staff
of his spear was like a weaver's beam, and his iron spearhead
weighed six hundred shekels; and a shield-bearer went before
him.

The fear I saw reflected in their eyes was a haunting reminder of a moment from my past, etched in my memory during a private audience with my father's flock of sheep. I vividly recalled the adrenaline coursing through my veins the day I stood paralysed, face to face with a massive lion that had set its sights on one of my vulnerable sheep, ready to claim its prey. I could relate, knowing we were facing a battle unlike any other. Yet, I stood firm but in awe, not at his sheer appearance but at his pompous words that echoed in my ears, filling me with anger and determination!

1 Samuel 17:10 (NKJV)
And the Philistine said, "I defy the armies of Israel this day;
give me a man, that we may fight together."

When I heard the pompous and blasphemous words coming out of the champion's mouth, who had been taunting the armies of Israel, my heart stirred with indignation. For 40 days and 40 nights, he unashamedly self-promoted his military experience. He paraded his trophies of battle with a swagger that seemed to mock not just the mighty men on the field but also the very heavens, defying the holy angelic armies of God, assigned for Israel's deliverance!

With the force and fury of a raging tempest, he called for a champion to represent our people; his voice was like the roar of a lion, commanding attention and striking fear into the hearts of many. The parallels between this moment and my past were striking as if history was repeating itself. I was transported back to the day I encountered the sound of a threatening and deep roaring growl coming out the mouth of a lion, a great distance from the flock, louder and louder as it approached my helpless flock. Though the lion is often deemed the undisputed king of the jungle, I learned on that fateful day that true sovereignty resides with One far greater than any king, champion or ruler. The same God who had delivered me in my youth, in the private audience of my father's sheep, could bring about salvation for His people once more.

Beloved, perhaps you will meet a giant that stands before you and your next season. How you carry yourself and what you do in that moment will create the subsequent trajectory of victory in your next season. Whether this giant is an illness, financial crisis, bereavement or spiritual conflict, it is not its strength and voice that matters; it is God's strength that can work through you!

Beneath the imposing grandeur of the champion's armour, I found my thoughts drifting back to a vivid encounter I once had with a wild bear deep in the untamed wilderness of Bethlehem. With its towering height, sharp teeth, thick coat, and long claws, the bear was a formidable sight. Similarly, Goliath, the uncircumcised Philistine, was like a bear making threatening gestures against the armies of God, his exorbitant armour only adding to the spectacle.

As I stood there, a profound realisation washed over me: this moment was a divine appointment orchestrated by God Himself! My father had entrusted me with food to deliver to my brothers, who were entrenched in combat at the front lines. However, in that instant, I wondered if there was a purpose far greater than merely satisfying their hunger. Could it be that God was positioning me not just as a messenger of provisions but for a battle I had faced several times when wild beasts would try to steal, kill or destroy my father's flock? It was a full circle moment, an orchestrated send-off from God, my heavenly Father, leading me to confront Goliath!

The private battles I faced with the lion and the bear to protect my father's sheep were not too far-fetched from this battle. When I finally listened to Goliath's taunting speech, I felt a strange calm wash over me. My past had been woven into this moment, giving me the strength and courage to face Goliath, unfazed by his size and boasts because, in private, I had fought a lion and a bear, who were just as bold, boastful, and large!

1 Samuel 17:25-27 (NKJV)
So the men of Israel said, "Have you seen this man who has come up? Surely he has come up to defy Israel; and it shall be that the man who kills him the king will enrich with great riches, will give him his daughter, and give his father's house exemption from taxes in Israel." Then David spoke to the men who stood by him, saying, "What shall be done for the man who kills this Philistine and takes away the reproach from Israel? For who is this uncircumcised Philistine, that he should defy the armies of the living God?" And the people answered him in this manner, saying, "So shall it be done for the man who kills him."

Midway in conversation with some of the men of war, my older brother found me. Unaware that our father had sent me to bring him food. He snarled at my intrigue and interest in seeking the welfare of Israel. He angrily charged at me, accusing me of pride, saying, "Why did you come down here? And with whom have you left those few sheep in the wilderness? I know your pride and the insolence of your heart, for you have come down to see the battle."

On the contrary, nothing about me in this situation was prideful except for Goliath and his lofty self-praises. Neither he nor Goliath's words could bully nor deter the determination in my heart to represent the army of Israel and fight the uncircumcised Philistine. Besides, there was a desperate attempt to woe any man to fight Goliath! Indeed, King Saul offered a three-part bribe, including a cash award, his daughter for marriage, and a tax exemption. However, this was not about material things or personal glory for me. It was about duty, restoring the dignity of God's people! A duty to disrobe the reproach, shame and fear that this uncircumcised Philistine had clothed the armies of Israel for the past 40 days and 40 nights.

1 Samuel 17:31 (NKJV)
Now when the words which David spoke were heard, they
reported them to Saul; and he sent for him.

In those pivotal and often challenging moments of transition in our lives, it becomes essential to discern when those who are nearest to our hearts may unintentionally lead us astray from the divine path that God has set before us—a path of faith that demands both courage and a steadfast sense of duty. I remember vividly how my oldest brother, despite his well-meaning intentions, tried to stop me from what I believed was God's cause.

So then, after they reported to King Saul, with both enthusiasm and uncertainty, the men quickly whisked me away to be clothed in Saul's armour, ready for battle with Goliath. Yet, as I stood there, clad in armour that felt ill-fitting, I realised it was not a suitable match for me. Each piece of the armour felt too large, too foreign, and ultimately too restrictive for me.

Beloved, have you been fighting battles with someone else's armour? Do you often try to mimic the

65

strategies and formulas of others in hopes of replicating their successes in your own life? That moment of grappling with ill-fitting armour before the battle was a profound lesson for me—it taught me an invaluable truth, that "I was enough!" God was able to use me with all my skills, talent and life experiences to overcome a champion like Goliath. Ultimately, it was not by my strength and wisdom that I would triumph, but His! Likewise, God can use you to overcome your own giants when you begin to disrobe from other people's pressures and expectations, along with envying other people to be willing to be authentic. I set my heart to use the same tools I used before when I fought and killed both the lion and bear.

1 Samuel 17:40 (NKJV)
Then he took his staff in his hand; and he chose for himself five smooth stones from the brook, and put them in a shepherd's bag, in a pouch which he had, and his sling was in his hand. And he drew near to the Philistine.

He stood there, towering over me and radiating with fury, behind an armour bearer who carried his imposing shield; he was insulted by my youth that a "small lad" was chosen to represent the armies of Israel and fight him. It was an insult to his manhood! His thunderous voice echoed off the rocky hills that framed the Valley of Elah as he cursed me by his gods. Though my voice in response was like a faint echo, a miniature growl compared to his, these words came from a place of deep-seated faith, surrender and trust in the God of armies! "You come to me with a sword, with a spear, and with a javelin. But I come to you in the name of the Lord of hosts, the God of the armies of Israel, whom you have defied. This day, the Lord will deliver you into my hand, and I will strike you and take your head from you. And this day I will give the carcasses of the camp of the Philistines to the birds of the air and the wild beasts of the earth, that all the earth may know that there is a God in Israel."

Unable to contain his anger, which was now boiling over, Goliath drew near to strike. Unprovoked, I ran towards him, reaching into my bag with the sling in the other hand. Those lonely nights I endured watching my father's sheep would account for this moment, that indeed, my Heavenly Father watches over His sheep. Running, I took a smooth stone and slung it towards him. It struck him in his forehead, and sinking in, he fell to the ground.

1 Samuel 17:50-51 (NKJV)
So David prevailed over the Philistine with a sling and a stone, and struck the Philistine and killed him. But there was no sword in the hand of David. Therefore David ran and stood over the Philistine, took his sword and drew it out of its sheath and killed him, and cut off his head with it. And when the Philistines saw that their champion was dead, they fled.

Discretion That Works With Opportunity

Before I had the chance to confront and ultimately defeat the formidable champion, Goliath, I had harnessed the ability to recognise and seize opportunities. In the lead-up to the battle, I took the time to articulate my personal victories, not out of a desire to brag or elevate myself above others, but rather to inspire confidence and gain the acceptance of those individuals in the position to appoint me as the figure to fight Goliath. This power of opportunity comes to each of us, inspiring us to seize our own God-given opportunities! It is a tragedy when one fails to recognise the rare opportunity to share their private victories. Yes, these moments are few and far between, which is why it's crucial to exercise humility and refrain from boasting unless the circumstances truly warrant such self-recognition.

1 Samuel 17:36-37 (NKJV)
Your servant has killed both lion and bear; and this uncircumcised Philistine will be like one of them, seeing he has defied the armies of the living God." Moreover David said, "The LORD, who delivered me from the paw of the lion and from the paw of the bear, He will deliver me from the hand of this Philistine." And Saul said to David, "Go, and the LORD be with you!"

In this current generation, conduits such as social media mean that you face far more temptation to unnecessarily share information before its time. Moreover, the universal challenge of not discerning and recognising the differences between private and public victory can lead to telling people things before their time. It's important to remember that the problem is not social media but pride, false humility, impatience, and lack of self-control hidden in one's heart. These are the driving forces for indiscretion. Practising humility, patience, and self-control allows room for awareness of the influence of social media; you can be more cautious in your sharing, fostering a more discerning approach.

Beloved, can you discern that every victory you've ever won doesn't necessarily need to be shared? Can you recognise how some of your triumphs may require a period of reflection, resting quietly on a special shelf within your heart until the right circumstances arise in your external environment to honour and validate your victory's narrative? Understanding the difference between a private testimony and a public declaration puts you in a position that demands you to foster care, intelligence, wisdom and vigilance because you now understand the sensitive connotation of your battle.

The man facing Goliath needed a unique resume showcasing military experience and courage. Therefore, I could leverage my private victories by sharing them publicly, aligning them with the current demand and need. I had to swiftly reassure these mighty men of valour in the presence of King Saul that I was no stranger to battle, with a resume that included slaying both a lion and bear. Beloved, is there a demand for you to share your life story? Is there room for your life story to inspire others into action?

Consider this, the bear and lion bestowed lessons and skills to enable me to confront Goliath as I did. Similarly, the lessons and skills you've acquired in the shadows will empower you to tackle more significant challenges in the open. These private battles make you a more audacious and fearless individual, ready to face society, financial markets, a global pandemic, a family crisis, or any other form of adversity! This is why discerning when to share your private victories is paramount.

If you have been fighting battles in private and winning them in an audience of a few or none, you are in good company! Are you waiting for someone to give you an inconspicuous standing ovation, recognition or a reward for your private victories? It may seem that no one can see you, including God Himself, but that private battle you overcome is a building block towards your evolving identity. Your private victories are not in vain; they are positioning you to identify a public battle you must fight! Moreover, every battle you won or lost was recognised by God, who is all-seeing and all-knowing. It will soon dawn on you why you had to go through what you went through when you fully come into your purpose.

Prayer

Heavenly Father, as You revealed strength, wisdom and fearlessness in the life of David when he faced Goliath, I pray that You also impart and reveal the same through me as I face my own adversity. Heavenly Father, I do not pray that You hide me from my giants but that I face them with Your power and endorsement. Today, fill me with the grace of discretion as You propel me into my place of purpose for this season of my life. I thank You that through Jesus Christ, I have already overcome my adversaries and that You will do exceedingly greater than I am asking now. In the name of Jesus, I pray, amen.

5. Nehemiah

Anyone With The Right Heart Can Rise Up To The Occasion

Sometimes, purpose shows up as a problem to resolve—one that no one else wants to tackle. For me, that purpose extended its arms wide open when I learnt of the state of Jerusalem. Its glory faded from its rich cultural heritage and revered godly history. The vibrant Jerusalem, a place of hope and divine promise, now stood in stark contrast to the crumbling remnants that were visible to all.

Purpose packaged as problems stood before me and I could not ignore it. I could not turn away from the reality that had been laid bare: our people had become scattered across distant lands, not because of political and military might but as a consequence of our collective disobedience to God's decrees. How could my heart bear this heavy sadness as I pondered on the fate of Jerusalem and my scattered brethren? The once-mighty walls of Jerusalem lay in ruins, and the charred remains of its gates served as a haunting reminder of our spiritual and moral decline.

So, I turned to God, seeking His guidance through fervent prayer and fasting. In the stillness of those moments, I poured out my heart, pleading for divine mercy, restoration, and deliverance. I yearned for us to be reunited as a nation and to rebuild what our sins had destroyed. As a cupbearer, I was in the service of the king, and I needed not only his favour but also his permission to embark on the task of rebuilding. This mission was not solely about my desire; it was about the restoration of a people, the revival of a heritage, and the rekindling of hope in a future that had been clouded by despair and uncertainty.

Nehemiah 2:1-5 (NKJV)

And it came to pass in the month of Nisan, in the twentieth year of King Artaxerxes, when wine was before him, that I took the wine and gave it to the king. Now I had never been sad in his presence before. Therefore the king said to me, "Why is your face sad, since you are not sick? This is nothing but sorrow of heart." So I became dreadfully afraid, and said to the king,

"May the king live forever! Why should my face not be sad, when the city, the place of my fathers' tombs, lies waste, and its gates are burned with fire?" Then the king said to me, "What do you request?" So I prayed to the God of heaven. And I said to the king, "If it pleases the king, and if your servant has found favor in your sight, I ask that you send me to Judah, to the city of my fathers' tombs, that I may rebuild it."

In this triumphant moment, not only did God bestow upon me extraordinary favour in the eyes of the king, but He also stirred the king's heart to respond with compassion and purpose. The king, recognising the importance of our cause, made the momentous decision to commission Calvary—a dedicated army of officers entrusted with the mission. Additionally, he ensured that I had the necessary resources to carry out this mission effectively, providing me with the means to turn aspirations into action and to lead our people toward a rebuilt city of Jerusalem.

Discretion Before Building

Nehemiah 2:11-12 (NKJV)
So I came to Jerusalem and was there three days. Then I arose
in the night, I and a few men with me; I told no one what my
God had put in my heart to do at Jerusalem; nor was there any
animal with me, except the one on which I rode.

When you are getting ready to build something, the last thing you want to do is publicly share the secrets in the frame of your mind and heart. The thought of exposing my innermost thoughts and the divine plans that God had instilled in me filled me with reluctance. I was determined in my decision to explore the gates and walls of Jerusalem without the interference of external opinions, unsolicited advice, or assistance from others. The pre-building part of this story was a personal journey, one that I wanted to navigate on my own until I felt fully prepared to absorb the magnitude of what lay before me. I carried discretion like a badge of honour, vigilant in safeguarding the sacred plans that pulsed within me. It was my responsibility to fully understand Jerusalem's devastated state before I could even begin to assess the cost and resources needed to construct the wall and gates of our glorious city. I told no one what my plans were, not even the Jews, priests, nobles, officials, nor those who were to do the work—until I had personally witnessed and felt the essence of Jerusalem's condition through my own eyes, heart, and mind.

Beloved, how do you see the state of what God is calling you to build or rebuild? Is your vision clouded by the critical lens of someone else's perspective? Do you find yourself calculating the emotional and spiritual costs of your aspirations through the filter of external voices, which can sometimes fill your heart and mind with fear, insecurities, and a lack of clarity? What is God calling you to rebuild in your own life today? Are the opinions, insights, and lived experiences of others skewing your vision, detracting from your focus, or hindering your ability to authentically build?

Sticks And Stones May Break My Bones, But Words Can Never Hurt Me

Grieved and profoundly distressed by the unsettling sights that had confronted me, I could not help but reflect on the unfortunate state of our beloved Jerusalem. It had transformed into a symbol of disgrace, and the weight of this reality bore heavily upon my heart. After witnessing the desolation and ruin firsthand, I finally mustered the courage to gather the officials of Judah—comprised of the nobles, priests, builders, and fellow Jews—to pour out my heart, despair and share my plans with them.

Nehemiah 2:17-18 (NKJV)

Then I said to them, "You see the distress that we are in, how Jerusalem lies waste, and its gates are burned with fire. Come and let us build the wall of Jerusalem, that we may no longer be a reproach." And I told them of the hand of my God which had been good upon me, and also of the king's words that he had spoken to me. So they said, "Let us rise up and build." Then they set their hands to this good work.

Before one builds anything of significance, one must always be prepared to encounter opposition. This resistance can come from unexpected quarters, often from those nearest to us—family and friends—which can wound us more deeply than attacks from outsiders. However, it can also stem from external parties who may feel threatened by your vision or mission. In our case, we faced ridicule from three prominent outsiders: Sanballat the Horonite, Geshem the Arab, and Tobiah, an official of the Ammonites. Not only did these men lack any personal or ancestral ties to the project we intended to undertake, but they also possessed no inheritance in the rich heritage that our efforts represented. When they caught wind of our plans, they reacted with open mockery, laughing with scorn and contempt, attempting to undermine our morale before we even commenced our vital work. They mocked our aspirations to rebuild the walls of our city, questioning our intentions with scornful and condescending remarks, saying, "What is this thing that you are doing? Will you rebel against the king?" The truth is that their actual discomfort lay in the fact that we were driven by a desire to seek the well-being of the children of Israel. Their mocking laughter was a thin veil for their apprehension, for they were deeply disturbed by our commitment to restore hope and welfare to our people, seeing it as a threat to their own positions and authority!

Beloved, have you ever found yourself in a similar situation where ridicule and scorn greet you even before you begin? What lies beneath the surface of their discouragement in you doing what God has put in your heart to do? It's essential to reflect on the deeper motivations behind such discouragement. Could it be that these adversities are orchestrated by Satan, who is trying to prevent you from making any steps, let alone from making meaningful progress toward your goals, especially those that promise to uplift and enrich your future?

Just like Sanballat, Tobiah and Geshem, you will find that discouragement and criticism often comes from those who who hold no meaningful role in your aspirations or projects. This is why you must judge and evaluate criticism through the lens of your purpose and vision in building. Some who criticise usually lack proper understanding of your mission or its significance. Purpose must always prevail above criticism. In our case, despite the taunts and mockery, we remained steadfast in our determination to not let their negativity deter us from our divine mission.

Nehemiah 2:20 (NKJV)
So I answered them, and said to them, "The God of heaven Himself will prosper us; therefore we His servants will arise and build, but you have no heritage or right or memorial in Jerusalem."

The Attacks Begin

Nehemiah 4:1-3 (NKJV)
But it so happened, when Sanballat heard that we were rebuilding the wall, that he was furious and very indignant, and mocked the Jews. And he spoke before his brethren and the army of Samaria, and said, "What are these feeble Jews doing? Will they fortify themselves? Will they offer sacrifices? Will they complete it in a day? Will they revive the stones from the heaps of rubbish—stones that are burned?" Now Tobiah the Ammonite was beside him, and he said, "Whatever they build, if even a fox goes up on it, he will break down their stone wall."

With determination and defiance at the core of our mission to rebuild Jerusalem, we would not be deterred by mere words from men who had no part in our inheritance! Beloved, this is the promise you can hold onto when you embark on the journey to fulfil what God has placed in your heart. Rest assured, He will orchestrate the arrival of dedicated individuals—both men and women—who are meant to support and uplift you as you progress in this divine work. Don't worry about who they are and where they will come from; as you take steps forward in faith and purpose, those individuals will emerge to seamlessly fit into the tapestry of your vision.

As we arrived in unity to start the great work, God began to raise specific men and women to move the vision forward, people equipped with unique gifts and experience, each aligned with the mission at hand. These were not just any random group; they included priests, merchants, perfumers, goldsmiths, and even the people of Zanoah, alongside the men from Jericho. Notable leaders, including one from the district of Jerusalem and his daughters, bravely stepped forward, joining hands to restore the gates and fortifications of our beloved city.

We meticulously restored and built the Sheep Gate, consecrating and hanging its doors. Also, the Fish Gate, with its beams, bolts, bars and doors, was laid and hung, and we fortified Jerusalem as far as the Broad Wall. Moreover, we repaired the Old Gate, the wall of Jerusalem as far as the Refuse Gate, the Valley Gate and the Tower of the Ovens, the Fountain Gate and the wall of the Pool of Shelah as far as the stairs that go down from the City of

David, the place in front of the tombs of David, to the man-made pool as far as the House of the Mighty, the place in front of the Water Gate toward the east, and on the projecting tower, the front of the Miphkad Gate as far as the upper room at the corner, and as far as the Sheep Gate.

United in purpose, we laboured in unity and purpose because the people had a mind to work, showing a steadfast commitment to the task. Together we constructed the entire wall, joining it up to half its height!

Nehemiah 4:7-8 (NKJV)
Now it happened, when Sanballat, Tobiah, the Arabs, the Ammonites, and the Ashdodites heard that the walls of Jerusalem were being restored and the gaps were beginning to be closed, that they became very angry, and all of them conspired together to come and attack Jerusalem and create confusion.

During the construction phase, we faced a series of attacks, predominantly verbal in nature–scorn, mockery and criticism. However, as we moved forward with the crucial work of repairs and restoration, the intensity of these verbal attacks escalated. It became clear to our opponents that mere words would not suffice to halt our progress. However, it was when the gaps were being closed, gates were being repaired, rubble was being removed, and the once-dilapidated structure began to reveal hints of its former glory that our enemies began to intensify their attacks! They understood that their verbal assaults were losing their effect. Beloved, when you build, it is vital to calculate not only the tangible costs of materials and labour but also the unseen costs associated with the inevitable conflict that often accompanies progress.

Nehemiah 4:11-12 (NKJV)
And our adversaries said, "They will neither know nor see anything, till we come into their midst and kill them and cause the work to cease." So it was, when the Jews who dwelt near them came, that they told us ten times, "From whatever place you turn, they will be upon us."

Prayer was a fortress throughout this work. Before reacting to our adversaries and the warfare they caused us,

I learnt the invaluable lesson of responding with prayer first. Discretion to not allow feelings and emotions to overshadow what truly matters in our mission. I realised that our enemies often sought to provoke emotional reactions, aiming to manipulate our responses and distract us from our mission. By choosing to lean into prayer and commit my heart to seeking God's face and direction during these periods of pressure, I found strength and clarity that enabled me to rise above their schemes. Dear one, effective prayer is a lifeline of hope that far outweighs man's counsel, for in prayer, we receive the very counsel of God. After prayer, I took strategic measures by appointing vigilant men to watch, day and night, over the work we had accomplished and what remained to be completed in Jerusalem. Despite the looming threat of violence against us from our furious enemies, we refused to let fear dictate our actions or halt our progress. We were determined to not let fear stop the work!

Nehemiah 4:13-15 (NKJV)

Therefore I positioned men behind the lower parts of the wall, at the openings; and I set the people according to their families, with their swords, their spears, and their bows. And I looked, and arose and said to the nobles, to the leaders, and to the rest of the people, "Do not be afraid of them. Remember the Lord, great and awesome, and fight for your brethren, your sons, your daughters, your wives, and your houses." And it happened, when our enemies heard that it was known to us, and that God had brought their plot to nothing, that all of us returned to the wall, everyone to his work.

An Unrelenting Pursuit

Our enemies of progress, driven by jealousy and a disdain for our advancements, came in full force when they learnt of our progress. Like predatory wolves on the hunt, they were relentless in their pursuit, eager to undermine the carefully laid plans we had set in motion. The moment they learned about the extensive repairs we had completed —most notably the reinforced walls that now stood tall and imposing, with only the gates waiting to be fitted with their doors—these foes intensified their efforts to thwart our progress. Indeed, they intensified their pursuit of me. In the heart of the day, when I was fully immersed in the tasks at hand, a sudden disturbance broke through the rhythm of our work. A group of messengers, dispatched by Sanballat and Geshem, arrived with an urgent message intended solely for me. Their arrival was a stark reminder of the threats we faced, yet fuelled our determination to press forward and complete our mission against all odds.

Nehemiah 6.2 (NKJV)
…Sanballat and Geshem sent to me, saying, "Come, let us meet together among the villages in the plain of Ono." But they thought to do me harm.

The mere thought of abandoning my work to meet with Sanballat and Geshem was quite baffling. How desperate had they become? Were they so driven by their agenda that they would go to the lengths of attempting to harm me or even kidnap me to impede the progress of our mission? Beloved, ponder this: how much will your success provoke the animosity of those who desire to see you fail? What depths will they sink to in an effort to stop the vision that God gave you? I had no intention of creating a scene or giving them the satisfaction of knowing their ploys affected me, for I would rather die than have left this great work to meet with the enemies of the Jews in a location as notorious as the plain of Ono, a place known for its association with compromise and betrayal.

Instead, I sent messengers to them, firmly stating, "I am doing a great work so that I cannot come down.

Why should the work cease while I leave it and go down to you?" In all this, I remained discreet with my communication, keeping the specifics of our construction project confidential, and safeguarding our strategies and timelines.

However, their determination was evident, as they sent the same request to me four times, each time proposing different days for a meeting. Yet, my response remained unwavering and consistent; I simply had no time to spare! Their persistence, while commendable, was not enough for me to conform even a minute of my time and life! Now, seeing that I was unwilling to halt this great work to dilly-dally and pause for their idle chatter, they resorted to a more cowardly tactic: they conjured up fabricated stories filled with accusations and insinuations. They sent an unsealed letter full of rumours, hoping that those who handled the letter would read it and also further spread these false rumours. Their ploy was calculated, as they aimed to provoke me into a meeting where we would supposedly discuss ways to prevent these deceitful stories from reaching the ears of King Artaxerxes. It was a clear effort to manipulate the situation to their advantage, leveraging fear and misinformation to undermine the work and welfare of the children of Israel.

Nehemiah 6:6-9 (NKJV)
In it was written: It is reported among the nations, and Geshem says, that you and the Jews plan to rebel; therefore, according to these rumors, you are rebuilding the wall, that you may be their king. And you have also appointed prophets to proclaim concerning you at Jerusalem, saying, "There is a king in Judah!" Now these matters will be reported to the king. So come, therefore, and let us consult together. Then I sent to him, saying, "No such things as you say are being done, but you invent them in your own heart." For they all were trying to make us afraid, saying, "Their hands will be weakened in the work, and it will not be done." Now therefore, O God, strengthen my hands.

Beloved, it is hard to build anything in fear. When fear takes hold, it disrupts your ability to build at a measured pace; you might hastily rush ahead, jeopardising the stability of your foundations, or you may falter and proceed too slowly, allowing doubt to undermine your efforts. Indeed, in moments of fear, one can overlook critical details—those small yet vital elements that, if neglected, can manifest as significant structural faults later on. Our adversaries understood the power of fear, recognising that by sending a menacing letter laden with threats, they could sap our strength and cause us to hesitate. This hesitation would compromise not only the speed at which we built but also our attention to essential details that ensure the integrity of our work. Building is more than mere strength; it also requires a foundation of peace, wisdom, unity, and vigilant awareness. If fear had infiltrated our hearts, it would have weakened these crucial pillars—our vigilance, unity and strength. With prayer as my crutch, I stood on it once again, placing my trust in God to safeguard us against the relentless attacks of the enemy. So I prayed, "O God, strengthen my hands!"

Amid the ongoing barrage of threats, my enemies resorted to more crafty tactics, employing a false prophet named Shemaiah, who was confined within his own home. However, when I went to visit him, expecting perhaps a word of encouragement or guidance, he instead delivered a message that was starkly misaligned with God's truth. He prophesied that my enemies were conspiring to kill me, suggesting that we should retreat and hide together by seeking refuge in the holy place of the temple. However, it is vital to remember that entrance to the holy place was strictly reserved for the priests of God. As I weighed his alarming predictions against the teachings of God, it became unmistakably clear that Shemaiah was not a messenger from the Lord. God's character is consistent; He does not contradict His own Word! It soon became evident that Shemaiah's prophecies were contrived. He was not speaking under God's divine influence but rather as a puppet of Tobiah and Sanballat, who sought to undermine my leadership through error had I entered the holy place, as I was not a priest! He pronounced this prophecy against me because Tobiah and Sanballat had hired him.

Beloved, it is essential to understand that if your adversary cannot overpower you through the conventional means of culture, society, politics or economic challenges, they may pivot to more covert tactics, utilising religious pretence or spiritual manipulation. This was their scheme: to use a false prophet to sow doubt and discord among the people, to tarnish my reputation within the Jewish community, to fracture our unity, and ultimately, to hinder the work we had set out to accomplish.

Discretion After Building

Nehemiah 6:15-16 (NKJV)
So the wall was finished on the twenty-fifth day of Elul, in fifty-two days. And it happened, when all our enemies heard of it, and all the nations around us saw these things, that they were very disheartened in their own eyes; for they perceived that this work was done by our God.

One of the most crucial times to exercise discretion and remain vigilant is at the very final stages of what you are building. It's essential to recognise that many people are often unaware of the subtle and deceptive tactics that can undermine their efforts. When someone finally sees the fruits of their labour take shape and witnesses their project come to fruition, it can be tempting to let their guard down, basking in the glory of their accomplishment and celebrating prematurely. This is because it is one thing to finish building but another to establish what you have built. It would have been foolish of us to celebrate now when we hadn't yet repented, consecrated ourselves, or gathered our people back from captivity.

Therefore, it's vital to remain composed and patient during the final phase, as the journey does not conclude with the completion of a construction. Yes, completion signifies an important milestone but does not equate to full establishment. Establishing what you have built requires ongoing effort, strategic planning, and continual vigilance. Beloved, discretion goes beyond the impressive structure you are erecting; it is an ongoing attitude of the mind that will keep you sober even after you have completed the vision God gave you. This ongoing attitude is critical, as it allows you to navigate through potential challenges and avoid complacency, ensuring that the foundation you have laid remains strong and resilient over time.

As I reflected on our progress, I was not unaware of the devices of Satan at work through Sanballat, Tobiah and Geshem. Disheartened by our completion they sent letters trying to frighten me in order to disarm our vigilance. These 'devices' are the cunning strategies and temptations that Satan uses to distract us in our walk of faith; fear and discouragement. Though we had finished building the wall—there remained a deeper issue at hand: my fellow countrymen were still scattered, spiritually fragmented, and disconnected from one another! We had successfully built and repaired the stones, doors, and hinges that would fortify our city, yet we were now confronted with an urgent need to address the spiritual condition of our hearts. Now, we needed to repair and rebuild our hearts that had been dismantled and scattered by the rot of sin.

However, it became increasingly clear that before we could embark on the internal work that would solidify our unity as a nation, I needed to exercise discernment. To safeguard our progress and prevent any potential sabotage, I applied discretion to stand guard, appointing guards from among the inhabitants of Jerusalem to guard the gates and doors of Jerusalem and keep them shut. This was not merely about protecting the physical structures we had built but was a vital part of preparing our hearts and minds for the work ahead. This internal transformation was essential before we could gather our scattered brethren back to Jerusalem. So then, we needed to collectively engage in true repentance, sincerely turning away from our sins and turning back to God. Consecration, setting ourselves apart for His service was paramount. Beloved, God desires you to not only build according to His good, acceptable and perfect will but He also wants you to be fully established once your building efforts have concluded. Through His grace and wisdom, you will be established to yield lasting fruit in your life and the lives of others.

Nehemiah 12:27-29 (NKJV)
Now at the dedication of the wall of Jerusalem they sought out the Levites in all their places, to bring them to Jerusalem to celebrate the dedication with gladness, both with thanksgivings and singing, with cymbals and stringed instruments and harps. And the sons of the singers gathered together from the countryside around Jerusalem, from the villages of the Netophathites, from the house of Gilgal, and from the fields of Geba and Azmaveth; for the singers had built themselves villages all around Jerusalem. Then the priests and Levites purified themselves, and purified the people, the gates, and the wall.

Prayer

Heavenly Father, I pray that you strengthen my hands to build the vision you have given me for the sake of Your kingdom and glory. Empower and enrich me with Your wisdom to finish this work in joy, peace and unity with those You bring into my life to help me. Father, I also ask that you establish me and this work I am doing, even as you did in the days of Nehemiah. This I pray in the name of Jesus, amen.

6. Samson

Discretion Comes At A Cost

Judges 13:5 (NKJV)
For behold, you shall conceive and bear a son. And no razor
shall come upon his head, for the child shall be a Nazirite to
God from the womb; and he shall begin to deliver Israel out of
the hand of the Philistines."

Some individuals are born with extraordinary gifts,

endowed with innate talents that distinguish them from

others. Some recognise their potential and actively seek to

enhance it by hiring skilled instructors who guide them in

honing their abilities. Others undergo rigorous training,

immersing themselves in educational experiences that

mould their skills over time. Then, there are those who,

through keen observation of others, seek out mentors to

help them refine their craft.

For me, my gift was given to me by God as He fearfully and wonderfully formed me in my mother's womb. It was a God-given gift that depended not only on God's power but also on my discretion to nurture, keep, and safeguard it.

James 1:13-14 (NKJV)
Let no one say when he is tempted, "I am tempted by God"; for God cannot be tempted by evil, nor does He Himself tempt anyone. But each one is tempted when he is drawn away by his own desires and enticed.

In the precedence of my gift, I became comfortable and grew increasingly complacent. I rose to be a judge, yet, naively, my judgement became clouded with a false sense of security in my gift rather than the gift-giver, God Almighty. I slumped deeper and deeper into my error. Many think that they can do whatever they want with their bodies, even when they are not married. However, the calling to be faithful does not only apply to those who are married.

Moreover, whether it's through sexual sin or addictions, to substance abuse, the calling to be faithful to your body applies to you. Faithfulness hangs on the hinges of holiness. I was unfaithful, neglecting the sanctity of my body and its calling to honour God. I sought solace in the embrace of various women, allowing myself to be swept away by fleeting pleasures, with each encounter further entangling me in a web of lust. One encounter after another, lust seized control, slowly unravelling the reins of my heart. Beloved, compromise guides us farther away from our destined paths. Sin will divert us from the purpose of our lives.

In my journey, I served as a judge for Israel, tasked with the solemn responsibility of delivering our people from the relentless oppression of the Philistines. This role was not just a position of authority; it was a sacred duty rooted deeply in my gift of immense strength, which was bestowed upon me by God. My gift of great strength was not merely for my own glory; it was intricately linked to the liberation of God's people and the execution of judgment with retribution upon God's enemies. However,

I found myself lacking the discipline needed to steward my own heart. Anointed and strong but I had become weak and vulnerable in the matters of love and desire. The void within me grew wider and wider, a hollow space that needed consecration.

Lust, once merely a fleeting temptation, had transformed into a compass, directing me aimlessly wherever my eyes might wander, a guide driven by the cravings of my body. I found myself lusting after the beauty of women in my heart, allured by their eyelids. Little did I know that I was courting danger; that by engaging with harlots, I was lowering myself to a mere crust of bread, thin and fragile, exposing myself to these strange women who one day would prey upon my precious life. At that point, I was deep in the realm of rebellion. It is around that season of my life, that I crossed paths with Delilah in the valley of Sorek. Pinning with desire, her name true to its meaning, is how she made me feel, a longing that could lead to my undoing.

With the object of my desire no longer above the heavens and the earth, my heart's desire was no longer fixed on my Maker. God was no longer at the forefront of my thoughts and affections. Beloved, this happens when the Author and Perfecter of your faith is no longer the focal point of your heart and existence. I found myself disarmed of God's discernment, discretion and wisdom that once guided my choices. My desire for sex and women had become the centre of my heart, and I had exchanged the virtues of discretion and chastity for fleeting pleasures, becoming vulnerable to my enemies who now lurked around me.

My love for Delilah was no secret. The flames of my desire for her were evident to those lurking all around me, a blazing fire that could not be concealed. The way I gazed into her eyes, the tone of my voice when I spoke her name, the tender brush of my hands as I held her when I touched her, all told a story loud enough to reach the attentive ears of the princes of the Philistines. They watched, recognising without difficulty that my heart and affections were set on Delilah.

Judges 16:4-5 (NKJV)

Afterward it happened that he loved a woman in the Valley of Sorek, whose name was Delilah. And the lords of the Philistines came up to her and said to her, "Entice him, and find out where his great strength lies, and by what means we may overpower him, that we may bind him to afflict him; and every one of us will give you eleven hundred pieces of silver."

Discretion That Comes At The Cost Of Chastity

I knew they were whispers that surrounded me—those hushed whispers that slithered through the air like shadows—but in that moment, I felt invincible. I didn't care. After all, I considered myself the pinnacle of strength, a living testament to the extraordinary gift I possessed. My gift had worked before, and it would work for me in moments of danger. When trouble arises, strength would come upon me, an army, even the formidable forces of the Philistines, could contain my strength.

The voices and opinions echoing behind my back, held little significance; what they said behind my back didn't matter to me as long as I was back in the bosom and lap of Delilah. My heart was anchored firmly in her embrace. Pride clouded my judgment, leading me to ignore those whispers rather than confront them. I continued to engage in a flawed union with Delilah, one that became increasingly troubling. She appeared to be more captivated by my extraordinary abilities than by me as a person—a realisation that lay heavy on my heart. Our once-sweet and enchanting fellowship and relationship began to be filled with tension and bitterness. In hindsight, I was guilty of the same. This is how I had treated the Sovereign God, focusing more on the manifestations of His power and what He could do for me rather than nurturing an understanding of His true nature; Majestic and Sovereign.

Judges 16:6-8 (NKJV)
So Delilah said to Samson, "Please tell me where your great strength lies, and with what you may be bound to afflict you." And Samson said to her, "If they bind me with seven fresh bowstrings, not yet dried, then I shall become weak, and be like any other man."
So the lords of the Philistines brought up to her seven fresh bowstrings, not yet dried, and she bound him with them.

Conversations turned from romantic to probing inquiries about where my strength came from. Delilah suddenly had a fascination with my past battles, victories and armour. I was in love, yet an unsettling question nibbled at me: was I a fool in love? The gravity of my situation worsened as I recalled her dealings beneath her affections. I knew that the 5 lords of the Philistines had bribed her each with eleven hundred shekels of silver (according to Jewish scholars, a shekel is equivalent to a day's wage in today's society). This staggering sum made it evident: Delilah was tempted by a price on my head, a price set by my very enemies.

Beloved, what price do you think Satan is willing to pay to stifle your voice and silence your divine calling? Always remember, your adversary is ever ready to leverage whatever resources necessary to impede you from working authentically within God's vineyard. Indeed, your adversary seeks to derail the kingdom work you are destined to fulfil.

Yet still, despite her pressing questions, Delilah's warm embrace enveloped me like a soft blanket, her intoxicating perfume tantalising my senses and her velvety skin igniting a fire deep within me. In that fleeting moment, I felt compelled to risk everything—a night spent in her presence, lost in the allure of her company. Lust had slithered into my heart, taking the seat at the centre of my heart, coiling itself like a viper, hissing its seductive whispers into my ear, slowly undermining the very discretion that had once served to safeguard my purpose and my precious gift. This venomous presence of lust pushed away the light of God's wisdom and clarity that had once defined my path.

Certainly, loss of spiritual focus is a heavy burden to bear, heavy and suffocating. Yet it is a burden that can only be discerned by one willing to confront their faults in humility. The weight of Delilah's daily pandering began to weigh heavily on me. Her voice began to haunt me, echoing in the quiet corners of my mind even in her absence; it was as though I had been bewitched by her persistence. Like an illusion, I would hear her voice echoing "How can you say, 'I love you,' when your heart is not with me? You have mocked me these three times, and have not told me where your great strength lies."

In the midst of her playful affections, she began pestering me daily with her words and pressed me so heavily that even my soul was vexed to death! I could see myself losing control in her presence, and finally I broke down and told her all that was in my heart.

Judges 16:21-22 (NKJV)

Then she lulled him to sleep on her knees, and called for a man and had him shave off the seven locks of his head. Then she began to torment him, and his strength left him. And she said, "The Philistines are upon you, Samson!" So he awoke from his sleep, and said, "I will go out as before, at other times, and shake myself free!" But he did not know that the Lord had departed from him. Then the Philistines took him and put out his eyes, and brought him down to Gaza. They bound him with bronze fetters, and he became a grinder in the prison. However, the hair of his head began to grow again after it had been shaven.

My fall was great but did not lead to my demise or total ruin. Though they took my sight, but with my life beyond the grave, I still had a voice. Yes, one that echoed with purpose and determination! Life in prison but not under 6 feet in the dust of earth presented me with an opportunity to mend my relationship with God. Beloved, it's never too late as long as you live, to seek redemption! I know that all things work out together for good for those who love God and to those who are called according to His purpose.

What the enemy intended for evil did not claim my life. Although they took my eyesight, I gained something far greater—an invaluable insight into God's intricate design and purpose for my life. I could now see clearly into my heart, free from the shackles of hypocrisy. Those eyes, which I had trained to chase selfish desires, were replaced by a new focus; my mind and soul were now attuned to see through the illuminating light of God's truth. Ironically, physical blindness became a catalyst for my transformation.

Though I was living in prison, entertaining the Philistines in their carousals, I was no longer imprisoned by lust and entertaining its thoughts. With a newfound focus, I began identifying everything within myself that did not align with God's will and purpose. I committed to a journey of change, meticulously picking apart the aspects of my character that needed refinement. In the absence of physical sight, I encountered repentance and made a heartfelt vow to live out the rest of my days, no longer driven by selfish needs but for the glory of God.

Judges 16:25-31 (NKJV)

Then Samson said to the lad who held him by the hand, "Let me feel the pillars which support the temple, so that I can lean on them." Now the temple was full of men and women. All the lords of the Philistines were there—about three thousand men and women on the roof watching while Samson performed. Then Samson called to the Lord, saying, "O Lord God, remember me, I pray! Strengthen me, I pray, just this once, O God, that I may with one blow take vengeance on the Philistines for my two eyes!" And Samson took hold of the two middle pillars which supported the temple, and he braced himself against them, one on his right and the other on his left. Then Samson said, "Let me die with the Philistines!" And he pushed with all his might, and the temple fell on the lords and all the people who were in it. So the dead that he killed at his death were more than he had killed in his life. And his brothers and all his father's household came down and took him, and brought him up and buried him between Zorah and Eshtaol in the tomb of his father Manoah. He had judged Israel twenty years.

Prayer

114

Heavenly Father, I thank You for the breath of life; I can make choices and decisions today that align with Your Truth and sovereignty. Father, forgive me for not living for you in the past. Today, I chose to commit my heart, strength, soul and mind to seeing You and no longer my selfish desires and needs. Thank You for ministering to me through the life of Samson as I learn from his mistakes. I pray You restore me discernment, wisdom, discretion and ability through Your grace and mercy. This I pray in the name of Jesus, the name above all names, amen.

7. Jesus The Christ

Love

1 Corinthians 13:4-7 (NKJV)
Love suffers long and is kind; love does not envy; love does not parade itself, is not puffed up; does not behave rudely, does not seek its own, is not provoked, thinks no evil; does not rejoice in iniquity, but rejoices in the truth; bears all things, believes all things, hopes all things, endures all things.

There are many reasons one may choose to be discreet: for self, others, or love. When the one I shared bread with had turned against Me, it was love that compelled Me to endure the pain of betrayal and disappointment, and keep discretion.

In a world that often prioritises exposure and public shaming, where relationships can become a cycle of retaliation and revenge, it is easy to take a detour from God's plan and purpose. In moments of betrayal, one might become so engrossed in the minor details of their hurt that they lose sight of the bigger picture. However, dear friend, facilitating the fulfilment of God's overarching purpose in your life—fuelled by love—is far more meaningful than giving in to the temporary discomfort of betrayal and heartache you may encounter. Exposing Judas was not essential to the narrative of Salvation, meant for all of humanity. Despite his betrayal, he played a role in fulfilling a more excellent plan, which culminated in My sacrifice on the Cross.

John 13:21-22 (NKJV)

When Jesus had said these things, He was troubled in spirit, and testified and said, "Most assuredly, I say to you, one of you will betray Me." Then the disciples looked at one another, perplexed about whom He spoke.

Can you see why exposing him to the other eleven would have derailed the unfolding events ordained for that night? Even after washing Judas' feet, demonstrating the importance of servanthood, and sharing a meal with him—dipping a piece of bread from the same dish—he remained captive to his own greed and motives. In the face of such betrayal, I chose discretion empowered by love, embracing understanding instead of anger and pettiness, by not exposing him to the eleven. The most impactful acts of discretion are those that stem from a deep well of unconditional love—agape love. This love calls you to rise above your hurt and seek a response that aligns with your life's purpose, allowing you to navigate betrayal with grace.

Grace And Truth

Luke 22:41-45 (NKJV)
And He was withdrawn from them about a stone's throw, and He knelt down and prayed, saying, "Father, if it is Your will, take this cup away from Me; nevertheless not My will, but Yours, be done." Then an angel appeared to Him from heaven, strengthening Him. And being in agony, He prayed more earnestly. Then His sweat became like great drops of blood falling down to the ground. When He rose up from prayer, and had come to His disciples, He found them sleeping from sorrow.

Flickering lights and serpent-like shadows weave among the tall trees under the full moon. The clamour of marching and footsteps drew closer; a garrison of men in formation, with Judas Iscariot leading the way. With the weight of the world on My shoulders, the hour of darkness had arrived. A stench of greed, lies and deceit introduced my adversary before greeting Me with a kiss on the cheek, a betrayal that echoed under the moonlight, intensifying the tension.

The crafty work of the Pharisees and chief priests was finally exposed through the heavily clad soldiers.

Their lanterns cast an eerie glow, and their weapons gleamed in the moonlight. Their lanterns illuminated their faces, revealing faces hardened by duty yet shadowed by fear. Beneath their breastplates and double-edged swords, they trembled like reeds in a storm; I saw the fragility of their hearts, devoid of truth, and the moral complexity that shrouded their actions.

John 15:13-15 (NKJV)
Greater love has no one than this, than to lay down one's life for his friends. You are My friends if you do whatever I command you. No longer do I call you servants, for a servant does not know what his master is doing; but I have called you friends, for all things that I heard from My Father I have made known to you.

For the last 3 years, I had become more than the LORD and Teacher to the eleven; I was a friend. More so, the Friend that sticks closer than a brother. This closeness was about to be disrupted, shaking the bridge we had built between memories and purpose in this hour of trial. Now, like a hen would gather her chicks under her wings, I stepped forward calmly, approaching the heavily armed garrison of men with Judas Iscariot, who were all unaware of the price I had just paid in the garden.

With all My heart and mind, I had surrendered to the Father's divine plan of Salvation—that through the ultimate sacrifice of My body, being nailed to the Cross and dying for the sins of the world; by faith, all humanity would be offered 'THE WAY' to Salvation and freed from the grip of everlasting death.

John 18:5-6 (NKJV)
Jesus therefore, knowing all things that would come upon Him, went forward and said to them, "Whom are you seeking?" They answered Him, "Jesus of Nazareth." Jesus said to them, "I am He" they drew back and fell to the ground.

When I revealed to them that "I am He," they struggled to receive the grace, strength, and peace that emanated from the sincerity of My words. My willingness to identify Myself startled them, and they stumbled over each other, falling like toy soldiers, rendering their torches, lanterns, and weapons useless. My heart was at peace, surrendered to the Father's perfect will, even as it seemed I was aiding in My arrest.

Again, not throwing discretion to the wind, being careful to emphasise that I am the One they seek. For I sought to forge a path of freedom for the disciples to escape being arrested. This cup of persecution was only Mine to drink. Yet, in this hour, their faith would be tested as they would witness a series of harrowing events: their beloved LORD being mercilessly beaten, scourged, and ultimately forced to carry the heavy weight of My Cross, culminating in My crucifixion and death upon that Cross before resurrection.

Confusion began to grip the disciples' hearts as they witnessed Judas's treacherous betrayal. Peter instinctively drew his sword in a desperate attempt to protect Me and regain control of the chaotic situation unfolding before them. With a swift motion, he struck out at Malchus, the servant of the high priest, cutting off his right ear in a moment of anger.

Matthew 26:52-54 (NKJV)
But Jesus said to him, "Put your sword in its place, for all who take the sword will perish by the sword. Or do you think that I cannot now pray to My Father, and He will provide Me with more than twelve legions of angels? How then could the Scriptures be fulfilled, that it must happen thus?"

With deep compassion within Me and My eyes fixed on Malchus, beckoning him to come closer, reaching out, I urge him, "Permit even this", and his severed ear was restored fully.

The soldiers were stunned into silence at this miracle. They did not understand that even in the face of trials, mercy triumphs over judgment. In the face of betrayal and injustice, the light of discretion can be shone through kindness, compassion and love. In a world of tit for tat, where one act of vengeance begets another, yet, deep within your heart are depths of love, ready for all to witness in times of strife.

Luke 22:52-54 (NKJV)
Then, Jesus said to the chief priests, captains of the temple, and the elders who had come to Him, "Have you come out, as

against a robber, with swords and clubs? When I was with you daily in the temple, you did not try to seize Me. But this is your hour, and the power of darkness." Having arrested Him, they led Him and brought Him into the high priest's house. But Peter followed at a distance.

Mercy

The sky hangs thick with dark clouds, and the sun's light escapes, struggling to be pierce through. Voices erupt around Me, chants, shouting and screaming. The crowds cry out, "Away with Him! Crucify Him!" A tumult of heated voices drowning one another in their fervent demand for justice.

John 19:16 (NKJV)
Then he delivered Him to them to be crucified. Then they took Jesus and led Him away.

On a stony and treacherous road, I carried My Cross. Many weary souls had walked this road. Yes, bloody stories have been associated with this way. This was no ordinary place; it held a legacy of suffering that echoed through the ages. Known as Golgotha, this hill carried a haunting resemblance to a human skull when viewed from a distance. It earned its name, "The Place of the Skull", for its shape and the dark history it embodied.

Here, on this cursed incline, the Roman authorities would bring criminals to face the ultimate humiliation and remind all of their military power. Criminals were stripped of their dignity; they were stripped bare and nailed to wooden crosses, their bodies exposed and vulnerable, left to die slowly in the unrelenting grasp of agony. In this dark hour, I became one of them!

The air was thick with the stench of blood and despair. With each step, the Cross became heavier. My body was weaker, battered and bruised as I bore 39 pain-searing lashes from the scourging and beatings they inflicted on My body. Yet, the Cross, heavy with its wood and bloodstains, was no match to the weight of the sin of the world I was determined to carry. With My heart resolute, I pressed on. I was resolved to shoulder this burden, to carry it until the very end, knowing that redemption lay at the culmination of this painful journey.

Isaiah 53:5 (NKJV)
But He was wounded for our transgressions,
He was bruised for our iniquities;
The chastisement for our peace was upon Him,

And by His stripes we are healed.

One nail, then two, followed by three and finally four. With each tap of the hammer, the echoes of each strike created a tense atmosphere. All around me, they stared and watched intently. In shame and humiliation, I hung on the Cross naked, with two criminals with Me, one on either side and I in the centre.

The Roman soldiers, carrying out the orders of their commanders, moved with determination. They did not know the weight of what they were doing, completely oblivious to the implications of their actions.

Dear friend, in our darkest moments, we must be willing to choose to see through the pain and anguish of other people's mistakes and reach out for forgiveness and mercy. Discretion, when driven by God's purpose, is choosing to forgive instead of being vengeful and letting resentment consume you. The soldiers, Jews and crowds hurled out curses, sneering and mocking Me. Yes, they pointed, jeered, and expressed their disdain. Yet, with all

My heart and mind, I had surrendered to the Father's divine plan of Salvation—that through the ultimate sacrifice of My body, death would no longer have power on those who would come to believe in Me. I prayed, "Father, forgive them, for they do not know what they do."

John 19:23-24 (NKJV)

Then the soldiers, when they had crucified Jesus, took His garments and made four parts, to each soldier a part, and also the tunic. Now the tunic was without seam, woven from the top in one piece. They said therefore among themselves, "Let us not tear it, but cast lots for it, whose it shall be," that the Scripture might be fulfilled which says:
"They divided My garments among them,
And for My clothing they cast lots."
Therefore the soldiers did these things.

Vultures fly above us, their beady eyes glaring with anticipation, waiting for life to leave our bodies before they swoop down and devour our flesh. The crown of thorns digs deeper into My temples. My face is bloody and unrecognisable. My body is bruised beyond recognition as My skin hangs like shreds from My ribs. My strength is dried up like a potsherd, and My tongue clings to My jaws. Piercing through the turmoil was a sound that tugged at My heart—a series of mournful cries. One voice stood out among the others, a familiar and heartbreaking sound that carried a depth of anguish. It was the voice of My mother, Mary, standing by John, filled with a depth of grief that only a mother could know. The day she greatly feared had arrived as she fought against the tide of despair that surrounded her, pouring out her love and sorrow for the one being unjustly condemned.

John 19:26-27 (NKJV)

When Jesus therefore saw His mother, and the disciple whom He loved standing by, He said to His mother, "Woman, behold your son!" Then He said to the disciple, "Behold your mother!" And from that hour that disciple took her to his own home.

In the midst of the torment and despair that enveloped Me, I bore the weight of anguish for the sake of humanity, even as the darkness deepened around Me. Knowing that every prophecy had been fulfilled and that My mission was coming to a close, with parched lips I spoke, declaring, "I thirst!" Now a vessel full of sour wine was sitting there; and they filled a sponge with sour wine, put it on hyssop, and put it to My mouth. So when I had received the sour wine, I proclaimed triumphantly, "It is finished!" And bowing My head, I gave up My spirit.

John 3:16 (NKJV)
For God so loved the world that He gave His only begotten Son, that whoever believes in Him should not perish but have everlasting life.

8. Ruth

My Past Does Not Determine My Future

A wise man once said that "our identity is not determined by the accident of race or nationality, but by the gracious act of God who called us to Himself." Yet, for me there are countless low seasons that I desired to have had a different nationality, race and ancestry altogether. Though my name is linked to Abraham the father faith, there was far too much shame hidden in the origin of my people, Moabites. Often bringing rejection and rift instead of welcome and peace. To understand my future I have to tell you about my past and my people, though my past could never vindicate me of my future. The background of my descendants is scarred by poor decisions, shame and incest.

Genesis 19:31-36 (NKJV)
Now the firstborn said to the younger, "Our father is old, and
there is no man on the earth to come in to us as is the custom of
all the earth. Come, let us make our father drink wine, and we
will lie with him, that we may preserve the lineage of our
father." So they made their father drink wine that night. And
the firstborn went in and lay with her father, and he did not
know when she lay down or when she arose. It happened on the
next day that the firstborn said to the younger, "Indeed I lay
with my father last night; let us make him drink wine tonight
also, and you go in and lie with him, that we may preserve the
lineage of our father." Then they made their father drink wine
that night also. And the younger arose and lay with him, and he
did not know when she lay down or when she arose. Thus both
the daughters of Lot were with child by their father. The
firstborn bore a son and called his name Moab; he is the father
of the Moabites to this day.

When God decided to bring judgment upon Sodom

and Gomorrah and the cities of the plain, seeing smoke

ascending towards the heavens, the daughters of my

forefather Lot likely believed in their hearts that God had

unleashed destruction upon the entire world, and they

were the only ones left! In ignorance, they played at the

drum of fear. They desperately devised a troubling

scheme, motivated by the desire to preserve their family

lineage. The sisters thought in their hearts, "Let us help

our father, but let us deceive him and lie to him". Hence, a narrative has transcended generations, leading many, particularly within the Jewish community, to perceive our nation's origins as stained by fear, deception, and the consequences of a lie. That our forefather Lot, had two illegitimate children, Moab and Ben-Ammi.

Beloved, reflect on your own life. Are you allowing ignorance to open a door to fear in areas of your life? Are you making life decisions out of a place of fear that is birthed from ignorance? Remember that God has not given you a spirit of fear but has given you a spirit of power, love and a sound mind through His Spirit and Word. It's essential to recognise that you are called to rise above fear, seeking God's truth and clarity in your choices.

The Flight Of Hope

Ruth 1:4-6 (NKJV)
Now they took wives of the women of Moab: the name of the one was Orpah, and the name of the other Ruth. And they dwelt there about ten years. Then both Mahlon and Chilion also died; so the woman survived her two sons and her husband. Naomi Returns with Ruth. Then she arose with her daughters-in-law that she might return from the country of Moab, for she had heard in the country of Moab that the Lord had visited His

people by giving them bread.

In the span of a decade, I transitioned from a life of luxury and privilege to a state of utter loss. Everything I had placed my hope in - my husband, aspirations to get pregnant and finally have children, a comfortable life, status, and faith in gods of stone made with human hands; was stripped away.

Like sheep searching for greener pastures, my late husband's family had left Bethlehem due to a famine, in search of better opportunities, eventually settling in my country, Moab, where I met him. He worked in pottery for the king, and life was perfect until sickness struck his body, and his brother's life was also destroyed. We went from a life of royalty to poverty and uncertainty. There were severe, tragic, life-defining moments that changed not only the trajectory of our lives but also the entire dynamics of our household. As the proverb warns, "Hope deferred makes the heart sick." My husband's noble Ephrathite name, once a proud symbol of our Jewish heritage and strength, gradually morphed to reflect the suffering we all faced. In that season of decline, Naomi had lost a husband and her two sons, whilst Orpah and I both lost a husband.

Looking at her with tears streaming down my face, I stood at the crossroads of my destiny. I faced a harrowing choice: to go with Orpah, who had decided to return back to her people and the familiar comfort of her gods, or to hold onto this woman who had been like a mother to me. With my hands trembling, I clung to Noami, my vision blurred by the bitter tears I shed, yet the bond we shared was crystal clear. Our shared experiences of discretion, joy, and sorrow had woven us together in a way that couldn't be broken.

Despite the overwhelming despair that had settled like a heavy fog upon Naomi's soul, transforming her from being pleasant to bitter, still, I couldn't bear the thought of parting from her! She may have seemed like a mere shadow of herself in the bitterness of her soul through tragedy. I clung to the belief in the Lord God she often told me about and the stories of her generous people in Bethlehem. There had to be a light at the end of this tunnel, and I was determined to find it with her by my side. In that pivotal moment, I surrendered my fears and doubts, placing all my hope in God.

Ruth 1:16-17 (NKJV)

But Ruth said: "Entreat me not to leave you, Or to turn back from following after you; For wherever you go, I will go; And wherever you lodge, I will lodge; Your people shall be my people, And your God, my God. Where you die, I will die, And there will I be buried. The Lord do so to me, and more also, if anything but death parts you and me."

Beloved, I urge you not to wait for a moment of crisis or tragedy to dedicate your life wholeheartedly to following God. Perhaps, like me, you've been walking a path that's not fully aligned with God, exploring and dabbling in magic, witchcraft, tarot cards, astrology, and crystals, while acknowledging God's name in public? Yet, it begs the question: is your heart truly given to God, or are you seeking answers, solutions and a sense of meaning in places that fall outside His embrace?

God desires so much more for you than a superficial acknowledgement. He longs for you to be fully immersed in His love, not because of fear but because He is the Lord and Master. He longs to walk in the fullness of His glory, to shower you with His blessings, and to reign in your life with His authority. More importantly, He desires to have a personal relationship with you, transforming you from the inside out.

Beloved, perhaps there are major life decisions you need to make, and it may seem like there are insurmountable barriers in your path. But God calls you to trust Him and align your actions with His instructions. Where there is God's instruction, there is undoubtedly God's promotion through obedience. However, He will not impose His perfect will upon you. It remains a choice that you must actively make for yourself, choosing to surrender your own will in favour of His.

Returning to Bethlehem evoked a flood of insecurities and shame I never experienced in Moab. This wave of emotions was not solely about my own feelings; it was amplified by my deep concern for my mother-in-law, Naomi. It was a humbling experience! Despite the warm welcomes from familiar faces, how could she begin to even articulate the magnitude of our shared loss? Instead of finding comfort in the familiar streets of Bethlehem and how God had shown mercy to its people, instead, the memories brought great distress and a deeper layer of grief to Naomi.

Moreover, as we walked through the town, I could see the toll this trip had taken on Naomi. Her eyes reflected not only the pain of our past but also the struggle of seeing those who had remained steadfast through the disheartening famine, clinging to hope in God while she had left for greener pastures. All this weighed heavily on her. This huddle was more difficult than I had imagined, seeing those who once knew Naomi unable to recognise her. It would soon dawn on all that she had left full and returned with a Moabite widow - no husband, sons, or grandchildren to speak of. The only solitary figure beside her was me—a Moabite widow with my own burdens to bear.

With the weight of responsibility pressing heavily on my heart, I faced a crucial choice. I could either succumb to the mourning and regret of what could have been in Moab and the husband I lost, or I could view this pressure as a call to revival. I chose the latter. I embraced a new mission. My commitment was now clear: I would find ways to care for Naomi, to support her in her time of need, and honour the bond we had forged through our shared trials. Our journey would not be easy, but together, we could navigate this path with God's grace.

Refuge In The Wings Of God

Ruth 2:1-2 (NKJV)
There was a relative of Naomi's husband, a man of great
wealth, of the family of Elimelech. His name was Boaz. So
Ruth the said to Naomi, "Please let me go to the field, and glean
heads of grain after him in whose sight I may find favor."
And she said to her, "Go, my daughter."

With hope in my soul and peace in my heart, the day had
finally arrived to leave the past behind and look ahead to a
future lived by faith. The deep sense of peace in my soul
was like a comforting blanket, wrapping me in its warmth
as I put on my shawl, preparing to go to the field to glean
heads of corn after him in whose sight I would find favour.
With Naomi's blessing, I set out to the field, my heart
brimming with expectation.

Yet, with each step I took and as the heat from the
fading morning sun surrounded me, thoughts of
discouragement, doubt, and worry began to invade my
mind, revealing the lingering insecurities within the depths
of my being. It was a battle to keep these feelings at bay,

but there was no going back; after all, I spotted a field from a small distance away. As I walked towards the vast field, the golden sunlight cast a warm glow over the young Hebrew men and women who were diligently harvesting the ripe corn. I felt a strong pull to join them and glean the leftover grain.

I made my way into that field and followed closely behind the reapers, carefully gathering the scattered grains of corn. Engrossed in picking the leftover heads of corn, I suddenly noticed a man near me, moving at a different pace than the reapers. Now standing up straight, I realised he was overseeing the workers, his keen eyes observing our every move in the field. I stopped immediately, mustered the courage to approach him, and asked, "Please let me glean and gather after the reapers among the sheaves."

His response of grace and courtesy settled my thoughts with stillness. With reassurance, I gleaned without fear that my distinct accent, unique skin colour, and unconventional behaviour would inevitably set me apart from the Hebrews as a foreigner. I embraced my differences rather than allowing them to isolate me. Though I kept our financial struggles and the sorrow of losing my husband hidden, I felt no shame; instead, I found a sense of ease even as I rested in the house with the other young women before I resumed gleaning.

As I continued gleaning, I noticed a distinguished older man making his way towards me. I would later learn that he was the master of the field, Boaz. His presence exuded authority, and his piercing gaze seemed to see right through me. He spoke words that opened a floodgate of tears within. These tears washed away the pain and doubts that had plagued my soul since leaving Moab. The healing his words offered was a gift of immeasurable value.

Ruth 2:8-9 (NKJV)

Then Boaz said to Ruth, "You will listen, my daughter, will you not? Do not go to glean in another field, nor go from here, but stay close by my young women. Let your eyes be on the field which they reap, and go after them. Have I not commanded the young men not to touch you? And when you are thirsty, go to the vessels and drink from what the young men have drawn."

At that moment, I had believed that I had gained the favour of the overseer of the reapers, but to my astonishment, it was the master of the field himself who had shown me favour! Despite keeping our life in Moab and my status as a widow entirely to myself, being very discreet, and the challenges I faced as a widow in a new land, Boaz demonstrated an understanding of our struggles and showed genuine empathy. Isn't it wonderful to know that our discretion also has a voice that will one day shout at the mountain of our hidden acts of kindness for all to see?

Ruth 2:14-18 (NKJV)

Now Boaz said to her at mealtime, "Come here, and eat of the bread, and dip your piece of bread in the vinegar." So she sat beside the reapers, and he passed parched grain to her; and she ate and was satisfied, and kept some back. And when she rose up to glean, Boaz commanded his young men, saying, "Let her glean even among the sheaves, and do not reproach her. Also let grain from the bundles fall purposely for her; leave it that she may glean, and do not rebuke her." So she gleaned in the field until evening, and beat out what she had gleaned, and it was about an ephah of barley. Then she took it up and went into the city, and her mother-in-law saw what she had gleaned. So she brought out and gave to her what she had kept back after she had been satisfied.

I fell to my feet, overwhelmed by the warmth of Boaz's presence. This man, whose age suggested he could easily be my father, spoke to me with such profound love, grace, honour, and dignity that I momentarily forgot my status as a foreigner, as someone who might usually be viewed through the lens of disdain, akin to a beggar or a slave. His words washed over me like a soothing balm, wrapping me in a sense of belonging that I didn't expect to find in this unfamiliar land. As if he was embracing me, I found great comfort in him and his words. I reflected on how the sincerity of my heart to care for Naomi and my acts of kindness within the four walls of our lodging had somehow reached the attentive ears and eyes of the master of the field!

Overwhelmed by this favour, I fully embraced this opportunity he presented to me—to stay in his field and glean among his young women and men. Boaz's kindness to me was not without coincidence; I would soon learn that he was a relative of Naomi.

Motivated by his generosity, I committed myself to working diligently in his field, resisting the temptation to wander elsewhere. I stayed close to his young women until the end of the four-month barley and wheat harvest.

Discretion That Fulfils Destiny

During these four months, I dedicated my time to working in Boaz's field. My primary motivation was to support and take care of Naomi, whose vulnerability during this time deeply touched my heart. Little did I realise that, in the midst of my labour and dedication to helping her, God was orchestrating events behind the scenes. He was actively overseeing and ensuring my security in addition to the favour I received in this field. How incredible it is to know that when we endeavour to secure the well-being of others, God, in turn, ensures the security of our own needs!

Ruth 3:1-2 (NKJV)
Then Naomi her mother-in-law said to her, "My daughter, shall I not seek security for you, that it may be well with you? Now Boaz, whose young women you were with, is he not our relative? In fact, he is winnowing barley tonight at the threshing floor.

As I prepared for this important night, I washed myself, taking extra care to ensure every trace of dust and weariness was washed away. I wore a new garment, my best one, to present myself humbly before the master's feet. As I anointed myself, the touch of pure olive oil on my head and hair seemed to tear away, from top to bottom, the garment of widowhood that still clung to my heart. With a sense of renewal, I made my way to the threshing floor, this time not to separate the wheat from the straw as done in the past but to be separated for God's divine purpose. This night held the promise of my destiny here in Bethlehem being fulfilled.

Naomi had been clear that I was to wait until the man had finished his meal and drink before I made my presence known. But it was more than just a physical waiting game. I had to quell the impatience and the desire to control the situation that bubbled within me. I had to surrender my plans, impatience and way of doing things and fully embrace the words Naomi spoke, allowing them to guide me through this night. Each step I took brought me closer to the threshing floor, a journey that mirrored the internal struggle I was facing. The chill of the night air wrapped around me, a stark reminder of my solitude, as I trekked alone under the blanket of stars. Was this really happening? A wave of disbelief surged within me; I had never done something so bold in my entire life! Was I being reckless to approach and lie down at the feet of a man, in such a manner?

Finally, I managed to make my way into the fields. As I journeyed to the threshing floor, I realised that this was not just a physical journey but a journey of dying to self. I arrived secretly, remaining hidden from view and ensuring that no one saw my face as I entered. Discreetly, I approached the threshing floor cautiously, not wanting to draw any attention to myself, especially from Boaz. I lingered around the threshing floor and watched as he skilfully winnowed the barley, taking in every detail of his movements. The night was growing darker as I patiently waited for him to finish his work and sit down to eat and drink. I continued waiting secretly as he ate and drank. I could not interrupt him until he was thoroughly pleased in his heart!

Still hidden, I carefully looked around the threshing floor where the process of separating the grain seeds from the straw would take place. As the night grew deeper, so did my patience. I remained patient and humble as the words of Naomi echoed in my soul. There, among the heaps of grain, with his heart merry, I noticed him reclining with a content heart. When he succumbed to sleep, I shifted softly towards him, carefully uncovering his feet. Like the scattered seeds of grain, I saw myself as a seed lying down, yet as if I had always been planted there, at the feet of the master. Quietly and patiently, I remained in that position for what felt like an eternity.

Have you ever wanted something so badly? Sometimes, in such moments, stillness is the only movement that matters. So, not letting my desire consume me, in still silence, I eagerly awaited him, my heart pounding with anticipation, knowing without doubt that his words would water the course of my life going forward.

Ruth 3:8-13 (NKJV)

Now it happened at midnight that the man was startled, and turned himself; and there, a woman was lying at his feet. And he said, "Who are you?" So she answered, "I am Ruth, your maidservant. Take your maidservant under your wing, for you are a close relative." Then he said, "Blessed are you of the Lord, my daughter! For you have shown more kindness at the end than at the beginning, in that you did not go after young men, whether poor or rich. And now, my daughter, do not fear. I will do for you all that you request, for all the people of my town know that you are a virtuous woman. Now it is true that I am a close relative; however, there is a relative closer than I. Stay this night, and in the morning it shall be that if he will perform the duty of a close relative for you—good; let him do it. But if he does not want to perform the duty for you, then I will perform the duty for you, as the Lord lives! Lie down until morning."

A Redeemed Ancestry

In the quiet hours just before the first light of sunrise broke through the horizon, I journeyed back to Naomi, my beloved mother-in-law. My heart sang with joy! How many nights I pondered, "Can a widow find love again?" The countless days I fought for strength to silence the voice of fear that threatened to paralyse me! My heritage, society, and beliefs burdened my shoulders with a weight I thought I could never lift. But there is a God whose arms are always open for us to find refuge in. As I made my way back to Naomi, memories flooded my mind, taking me back to the moment she had returned to Bethlehem with me. It was a time when I first dared to put my trust in God, taking refuge in Him in an unusual journey to a people I did not know and a life I had to adapt to. That daunting day, stepping out alongside my mother-in-law, unknowingly placed me in the perfect will of God. His will that would bring about my redemption! It was astonishing to realise that there were ten generations from the generations extending back to Lot all the way to the man who could become my kinsman-redeemer, Boaz. I reflected on my own identity as a Moabite—a foreigner, an outcast.

I was not entitled to an inheritance from Naomi nor anything pertaining to the Commonwealth of Israel and certainly not Israel's barley harvest; I was a Gentile. Taking the steps of faith conveniently brought me into a household now cleansed of a curse spanning through 10 generations! That is, 10 generations of Moabites and Ammonites being banned from the Assembly of God; the presence of Jews. Coming with Naomi to Bethlehem entered me into the Assembly of the Lord at the right time, place, and generation! Was it a coincidence that I came to Bethlehem in this generation? No, this decision was not a mere coincidence but a redemption orchestrated by the hand of God. Yet, this was not just about the redemption of my love story but also of my nation, the Moabites. Indeed, the decision to follow Naomi was not just a personal choice but an act of faith on my part and also obedience to God's plan.

As I hurried into the city, the sun hovered above the horizon, casting golden hues across the sky. I moved swiftly, careful to remain unnoticed until I could gather my thoughts. Deep within my heart, I held onto the oath of redemption from the master! I was confident that his word would come to pass sooner rather than later as I recalled how he esteemed me as a woman of noble character. Although he had mentioned a relative closer than him whose right was to redeem the property and marry me. Yet, the thought that I, once like a slave, could become the master's bride lingered in my soul. The prospect of transitioning from a life of scarcity to fully inheriting the abundance that belonged to the master filled my heart with uncontainable joy.

I rushed to the place and carefully placed the 6 ephahs of barley that Boaz had generously given me. They were valuable, worth at least three months of wages, and symbolised Boaz's commitment and provision for us. I turned to look at my mother-in-law and couldn't contain my emotions. I fell into her arms and poured out everything that had happened and all the thoughts and feelings weighing on my heart.

Ruth 3:17-18 (NKJV)

And she said, "These six ephahs of barley he gave me; for he said to me, 'Do not go empty-handed to your mother-in-law.'" Then she said, "Sit still, my daughter, until you know how the matter will turn out; for the man will not rest until he has concluded the matter this day."

Now, to understand my future, I have to tell you about Boaz's background. Similarly, like my ancestry, scarred by wrong choices, lust and sin, God's redemptive grace was working its way through the veins of his marred ancestry, going back to Judah, one of the twelve sons of Jacob.

Genesis 38:6-11 (NKJV)

Then Judah took a wife for Er his firstborn, and her name was Tamar. But Er, Judah's firstborn, was wicked in the sight of the Lord, and the Lord killed him. And Judah said to Onan, "Go in to your brother's wife and marry her, and raise up an heir to your brother." But Onan knew that the heir would not be his; and it came to pass, when he went in to his brother's wife, that he emitted on the ground, lest he should give an heir to his brother. And the thing which he did displeased the Lord; therefore He killed him also. Then Judah said to Tamar his daughter-in-law, "Remain a widow in your father's house till my son Shelah is grown." For he said, "Lest he also die like his brothers." And Tamar went and dwelt in her father's house.

They say it was a cold and empty night; the stars seemed to have fled the sky as thick clouds enveloped around the bright shining moon. Anger, resentment and deferred hope grew in Tamar's heart, dashing her hope. Thoughts of having her promised husband were further slipping away. Instead, a new desperation spread in her heart to secure her future. Governed with retribution, she sought for security guise of revenge. She was a woman cornered by society's expectations and her own unfulfilled dreams. Determined in her heart, she resorted to harlotry. A security that came at the cost of her dignity and womanhood. She disguised herself as a prostitute to secure her future.

Tamar is not too different from me. I know the hopeless nights and the pain of being a widow. I can relate to her pain because I know the grief of mourning for a husband. I, too, once sought security, but I found mine under the wise counsel of my mother-in-law, Naomi. One can say that the wise counsel I received is what separates me from Tamar. If only there was someone there to guide Tamar in wise counsel when she realised that Shelah had grown up and she had not been given to him as his wife.

Beloved, are you seeking for your own security too today? At what cost will you obtain it? Wise counsel can establish your security for generations to come! Life will deal each of us seasons of retribution but it is how you go about attaining your justice. For the sake of tomorrow, let yours be founded on Truth! Tamar's drastic measures, which led to illegitimate children, are a lesson for you about the consequences of seeking security at any cost and the importance of wise counsel in making decisions.

Notwithstanding Judah drowning in grief and mourning the loss of his wife, he did, however, under the guise of self-gratification, selfishness and lust, commit sin with Tamar. Though he was misled by her disguise, thinking she was a harlot, unaware that it was his daughter-in-law. In the end, Tamar conceived and bore twins. The problem is that the children would be illegitimate according to the law, having no inheritance until the 10th generation.

Deuteronomy 23:3 (NKJV)
"An Ammonite or Moabite shall not enter the assembly of the Lord; even to the tenth generation none of his descendants shall enter the assembly of the Lord forever,…"

[Forever in Hebrew is **aeon** which also means ages or a concealed time]

This error between Judah and Tamar directly affected the prophetic Word spoken over Judah by Jacob (see Genesis 49:9-10). Jacob prophesied that from Judah would emerge a lineage of kings. Yet, Judah was careless with who he gave his seed, careless enough to sleep with a harlot, though the harlot would turn out to be his daughter-in-law.

Are you mindful or careless with the things God gave you that have the potential to grow into greatness? His illegitimate children would have no inheritance until the 10th generation. Indeed, after Boaz, a young boy named David, my grandson, would be born and anointed to be king, fulfilling the prophetic Word over Judah's life.

Matthew 1:3-6 (NKJV)

Judah begot Perez and Zerah by Tamar, Perez begot Hezron, and Hezron begot Ram. Ram begot Amminadab, Amminadab begot Nahshon, and Nahshon begot Salmon. Salmon begot Boaz by Rahab, Boaz begot Obed by Ruth, Obed begot Jesse, and Jesse begot David the king.

Beloved, do you know that your actions today can affect the prophetic Word spoken over you? Sometimes, you need to meet certain conditions in order for God's perfect will to come to pass in your life. God's Word over you needs the right conditions to flourish! Moreover, there are conditions of discretion that will sit on your shoulders as you navigate through the prophetic Word spoken and written over your life. Hence, why you need to uphold and value what God has said about you. Boaz's past and family were not perfect, nor mine, but God's grace and mercy brought us together to fulfil God's plan.

Destiny Fulfilled

Time seemed to stall as I wondered in my heart what my life could become. The echo of my master's voice and words was now all etched into my heart as I waited for the fulfilment of what I was destined to become: a wife again and a mother. Indeed, a bride to the master of the field and a mother who would birth kings. No longer would I be a widow from Moab. Like the closing of a curtain, it felt as though my story was on the verge of a dramatic transformation.

Little did I realise that on that very morning, Boaz, guided by wisdom and discretion, wasted no time. He swiftly went to the city gate along with 10 elders and engaged in a conversation with his close relative, who ultimately agreed to redeem the land but declined to take me as his wife for reasons I'm grateful to not know! So then, Boaz bought everything that was Elimelech's, Chilion's and Mahlon's, including marriage to me, in order to preserve the family name in Israel. Following Jewish custom, the relative confirmed the transaction by giving his sandal to Boaz, who then announced to the elders and the people that he had acquired the property and would marry me!

Throughout this process, Boaz showed a remarkable blend of discretion and grace. He acted with integrity, choosing not to improperly pursue my request for marriage before ensuring that his close relative, who had the first right to redeem me, was given a chance to make his own choice. Moreover, he had privately gone to gather 10 elders to speak with his relative before publicly declaring to all the people and the elders his plan to marry me.

Beloved, through God's mercy and obedience to His will in going to Bethlehem with Naomi, I immediately became engrafted into the lineage of the master, Boaz, and ultimately, into the greater heritage that pointed toward the Master and Lord of lords, Jesus Christ.

Ruth 4:13 (NKJV)
So Boaz took Ruth and she became his wife; and when he went
in to her, the Lord gave her conception, and she bore a son.

Prayer

Heavenly Father, You are the giver of all wisdom. From the beginning of time, You have established all things, including every aspect and detail of my life. I ask You for wisdom to be kind, faithful and discreet as I manage all the details of my life, both things I can see and things I cannot see. Teach me to trust You for my best as I grow in this wisdom you have granted me today. I thank You for this wisdom that will grow from grace to grace and that You will fulfil every good thing You have ordained for me to walk into in this life. I ask for Your forgiveness for every plan I sabotaged through impatience, lust and selfishness. Restore me today, as You did for Ruth according to Your riches in grace. This I pray in Jesus' name, amen.

9. Elizabeth

Times And Seasons

Luke 1:5-7 (NKJV)
There was in the days of Herod, the king of Judea, a certain priest named Zacharias, of the division of Abijah. His wife was of the daughters of Aaron, and her name was Elizabeth. And they were both righteous before God, walking in all the commandments and ordinances of the Lord blameless. But they had no child, because Elizabeth was barren, and they were both well advanced in years.

The pain of waiting had gone over the threshold of my body such that it felt like it was choking my soul. Year after year, my husband and I found ourselves immersed in ministry, serving our community and witnessing families who came to present and dedicate their newborn babies to the Lord. My husband, a devoted priest, embraced each family with genuine warmth; his voice, filled with love and hope, offered blessings that resonated deeply. Yet, behind his reassuring smile and uplifting words lay a shared grief that echoed through our hearts. Our bond, tested by the weight of our unfulfilled dreams, only grew stronger as we navigated this painful journey together. Indeed, it is possible to mourn for a future that remains just out of reach, a future you know you are entitled to, grounded in the good deeds and faith you have upheld. You see, I did not wear any widow garments, but my heart was draped in garments of mourning that grieved not only what could have been but also what still might have never been.

Every time I looked in the mirror, I could almost hear the once-vibrant clock of time begin to quiet; each tick was a painful reminder of the dreams that felt increasingly out of reach. The once smooth contours of my face were now marked with deepening wrinkles, a testament to the months and years that slipped away, and the glow in my heart became stone-cold in the face of ridicule and scorn. To feel hope again for a child of our own was a luxury, a distant dream that seemed to slip further away as time marched on. Age had begun to catch up with my husband and me, casting shadows over the fervent wishes we once held close. Conceiving and nurturing the baby boy I had often envisioned—the little one who frequently filled my dreams and visions—now felt like a haunting memory rather than an anticipated future. Could a woman my age bear children? I wondered as doubt crept into my mind. I had faith in God's ability but had no hope in my circumstances. The future we so desperately desired for ourselves, having our own child, seemed impossible! The longing for motherhood was a constant ache in my heart, a yearning that seemed to grow with each passing day as I wrestled with the reality of my dreams turning to dust.

Luke 1:37 (NKJV)
"For with God nothing will be impossible."

The guilt of my perceived failure, not being able to give my husband a child, pressed heavily upon my heart like a sack of rocks that burdened my every breath. In a godless society, with all our hearts, my husband and I strive to live a godly life. Despite living in a world that seemed increasingly devoid of godly principles, my husband and I dedicated ourselves wholeheartedly to embodying a righteous life. We adhered strictly to the texts and teachings of the law, following the guidelines laid out for us as devout individuals seeking to please God.

However, the reality outside our home told a different story, casting shadows over our intentions. The absence of a child felt like a cruel judgment upon us. It was believed, almost universally, that such a blessing was reserved for those who had proven themselves worthy through righteous living—a belief that weighed on us painfully. As faithful servants of God, we bore the weight of this misconception. Whispers spread like wildfire, and soon, the chilling speculation took root among our peers. It was unsettling to witness their judgments. Even those who had once stood by our side in fellowship began to scrutinise our lives, attributing our childlessness to some grave sin we must harbour in secret. Dissecting the cause of our so-called "disapproval from God" became so absurd, even implying that Zacharias had stolen me from his brother many years ago!

Leviticus 20:20-21 (NKJV)
If a man lies with his uncle's wife, he has uncovered his uncle's nakedness. They shall bear their sin; they shall die childless. If a man takes his brother's wife, it is an unclean thing. He has uncovered his brother's nakedness. They shall be childless.

Such tales became a source of twisted entertainment for some, sowing divisions within our community and making a spectacle of our intimate struggles. Their condescending assumptions created an air of stupor around our house, marriage and devoted ministry. The weight of these assumptions was suffocating. I became the embodiment of disgrace—the barren wife of a priest, branded by labels and judgments that no amount of faith or devotion could erase. The walk of faith and ministry we had devoted ourselves to felt overshadowed by the stigma of our situation. As the whispers intensified, I began to question not only how others saw us but also how we saw ourselves in God's eyes. Yet, even in all this, I did not grow bitter.

The echoes of snickering, the hushed whispers, and the piercing stares that had haunted us over the years gradually chipped away at the fragile remnants of hope I clung to. I could vividly remember the cruel remarks that floated through the air like poisoned arrows. "Hahaha, did you see Zachariah today dedicating yet another child? Is he not ashamed of his sins?" they would jeer, their laughter ringing in my ears long after their voices faded. In those moments, it often seemed as though my ability to feel, yes, the flickers of joy and warmth in my heart was drowned by the noise of people's judgement. Yet, deep within the depths of my soul, a stirring began; a quiet sense of defiance whispered that perhaps all was not lost!

And just when despair threatened to take hold completely, an unexpected shift was on the horizon. God was about to intervene in a magnificent way, ready to bestow blessings upon me, an ageing and barren wife who had faced the scorn of many. There is a time and a season for everything under the heavens, even when we do not perceive it. This moment, long-awaited and fervently prayed for, was poised to pierce through the thick darkness that had enveloped my existence for far too long.

Luke 1:8-16 (NKJV)

So it was, that while he was serving as priest before God in the order of his division, according to the custom of the priesthood, his lot fell to burn incense when he went into the temple of the Lord. And the whole multitude of the people was praying outside at the hour of incense. Then an angel of the Lord appeared to him, standing on the right side of the altar of incense. And when Zacharias saw him, he was troubled, and fear fell upon him. But the angel said to him, "Do not be afraid, Zacharias, for your prayer is heard; and your wife Elizabeth will bear you a son, and you shall call his name John. And you will have joy and gladness, and many will rejoice at his birth. For he will be great in the sight of the Lord, and shall drink neither wine nor strong drink. He will also be filled with the Holy Spirit, even from his mother's womb. And he will turn many of the children of Israel to the Lord their God.

Discretion In Face Of Miracles

Luke 1:21-23 (NKJV)
And the people waited for Zacharias, and marveled that he lingered so long in the temple. But when he came out, he could not speak to them; and they perceived that he had seen a vision in the temple, for he beckoned to them and remained speechless. So it was, as soon as the days of his service were completed, that he departed to his own house.

When the man of God returned after a week, our lives took a dramatic turn that would alter our existence forever. It was an unexpected shift because as he attempted to reclaim the familiar rhythm of his speech, he struggled to articulate himself as he once did. In sync with his silent battle, I, too, struggled. I found myself grappling with my own rhythm of the body, feeling disoriented and amplifying a sense of helplessness that I had never known before. The nausea surged within me, and an overwhelming tiredness clung to my bones, rendering me weak and out of control.

So then, our communication had transformed entirely; we were learning a new language, one without the comfort of words. I also found myself navigating uncharted waters as I sought to decipher the cryptic signals my ageing body was sending me. A whirlwind of emotions swirled within me—excitement, terror, and sheer exhaustion all intertwined into a single overwhelming experience.

For the first few weeks, I wandered through the quiet hallways of both my home and my mind in a haze of disbelief, reconciling myself to the staggering reality that this was indeed a possibility. My body, now well past its youthful vigour, responded to the unfolding situation with symptoms that were all the more intense. It felt as if I became mute like Zacharias, astonished and filled with awe at the undeniable evidence of what we had once so desperately hoped for—against all odds, I was with child! How could I possibly explain the extraordinary situation of a woman who had entered her golden years and was well into the throes of menopause, suddenly finding herself pregnant? The only answer lay in the undeniable truth that this was nothing short of a miracle from God!

Beloved, have you ever longed for something so desperately that, when it finally graced your life, you found yourself at a loss for how to truly accept it? The signs were unmistakable; it was clear that God had graciously opened my womb and bestowed upon me the incredible miracle of conception. In this particular season, Zacharias and I experienced a deepening unity beyond anything we had encountered before. Words became unnecessary; the depths of his joy, love, and anticipation for the miracle growing within me spoke volumes through the warmth of his embraces and the spark of faith in his eyes.

A newfound sense of joy and peacefulness, which I had long sought after, began to take root in my heart, gradually erasing the years of tears, anxiety, and anguish that had burdened my soul.

On the other hand, Zachariah's sudden loss of voice ministered to my spirit in a way I could not have anticipated. God had lovingly silenced him as a means of safeguarding His word, preserving both Zacharias and our miraculous baby—his mouth was sealed due to a lack of belief in the fulfilment of what the angel had proclaimed. This served as a sobering reminder of the delicate nature of discretion, not only in our words but also in our actions. It instilled within me a sense of caution, urging me to be equally absent from the prying eyes of those who surrounded us. Yes, it was essential to retreat from the scrutiny for as long as necessary! For the sake of our miracle, I could not risk inviting doubt into our sacred journey.

So then, while my husband's voice remained absent, I chose to conceal my presence, exercising wisdom in the decision to keep my pregnancy under wraps rather than shouting it from the rooftops. I resolved to conceal this blessing as long as possible, waiting until the risks of a miscarriage were significantly reduced. Thus, I cloaked myself in discretion, vanishing from public scrutiny; I remained hidden for five months, allowing faith and hope to flourish in the silence.

Luke 1:24-25 (NKJV)
Now after those days his wife Elizabeth conceived; and she hid herself five months, saying, "Thus the Lord has dealt with me, in the days when He looked on me, to take away my reproach among people."

Beloved, it is essential to recognise that countless men and women have unwittingly opened the door to danger within their homes. This often stems from an inability or unwillingness to keep joyful news private until the hand and footprint of their blessing are formed? Did you know it takes 5 months for a baby's hand and footprint to be formed in the womb? Many find it difficult to keep their blessings private until those blessings have fully matured and established a clear identity. Understandably, it can be incredibly challenging to exercise discretion, especially when overwhelmed with joy and anticipation for what is to come. However, maintaining a certain level of confidentiality can serve as a vital foundation for safeguarding our blessings, withstanding scrutiny, pressure and comments from the outside world.

For instance, if I had openly celebrated my pregnancy the moment I discovered it, driven by a desire to respond to those who had once laughed and mocked us in our journey through childlessness, I would have opened the door to even more unwarranted scrutiny. Such scrutiny could have jeopardised our faith and the joy we ultimately experienced in welcoming a child later in life. This was an unusual miracle, and it deserved the reverence and careful consideration it commanded. It is essential to remember that some miracles require a delicate approach; they are gifts from an extraordinary God that need to be shared at the right moment and with the right people (see Luke 1:26-38). It is prudent to let our blessings grow and flourish out of the public eye until they are ready to thrive in their full glory.

Prayer

Heavenly Father, I humbly ask for your forgiveness for my past carelessness with the blessings I lost before birthing them due to my careless words and actions. I am grateful for the lesson I learned from the life of Elizabeth, as shown in the scriptures, about discretion and the importance of discerning the weight and value of what I carry. I pray that with Your wisdom, I can discern each seed of conception You entrust me with today and for the rest of my life. Teach and power me to nurture, maintain and edify what You give me as You make it to grow. This I pray in the name of Jesus, amen.

10. Conclusion

What have you learnt about yourself and about God ways and plans, from the 9 chapters in this book? What tools of encouragement have you taken with you to begin a new journey as you apply these principles of discretion? Take it one step at a time and be consistent as the Holy Spirit continues to reveal to you the art of being discretion according to God's will for you!

I pray that every form of blindness that you had before reading this book was removed through the Blood of Jesus Christ and that daily you will fill yourself with Jesus through His WORD, which sets you free. I pray that every chain of imprisonment that was entangling you was broken by the anointing of God, the Holy Spirit.

Beloved, if you have not yet given your life to Jesus the Christ, you are missing out on real love, hope and peace that transcends all understanding. It's written:

Romans 10:9 (NKJV)
"…that if you confess with your mouth, "Jesus is LORD," and believe in your heart that God raised him from the dead, you will be saved."

Just believe in your heart today that Jesus is the Son of God and confess it with your mouth. Say "Jesus I believe You are the Son of the living God, today be the Lord and God of my life and teach me Your ways daily by Your Spirit, fill me right now with Your Holy Spirit in Jesus name, Amen."

You are now a new person in Christ, forgiven and sanctified! Now purchase a Bible in the NKJV, if you don't already have one and beginning with the book of John read all through it. Read also Luke, Mark and Matthew and all the way to Revelations. Afterwards, you can then read from the book of Genesis up to the book of Matthew. Begin to study your Bible daily to know who Jesus is and who you are in Him. Even if it means being secluded from the world and from your friends for a time, even if they mock you, believe me, knowing who you are first through knowing who Jesus is, is more important than anything in the world.

Lastly, although there are many online Bible teachings including Bible study teachings that I personally do every Wednesday (via my youtube channel - youtube.com/@dephneaviyah), I, however, strongly recommend that you find a sound bible-teaching local church, ask your relatives or friends where they attend church and then start attending church services, Bible studies and prayer meetings so that you can grow as you fellowship with others.

The grace of our Lord Jesus Christ, the love of God and fellowship of the Holy Spirit be with you today and forever. Amen. God bless you.

In His service

Dephne Victorious Aviyah

Acknowledgements

To my beautiful family, my husband Lloyd, son Gabriel and daughter Anna-Ciyona. You are my wealth and blessings on earth and I am incomplete without you all. Thank you for inspiring and allowing me to thrive in my God-given gifts. I love you all deeply.

References

www.biblegateway.com

https://www.blueletterbible.org/

https://www.dictionary.com

https://www.merriam-webster.com/

Bruce, F.F. (2008) Zondervan bible commentary: One-volume illustrated edition. Zondervan.